the SELF LOVE WORKBOOK

*a life-changing guide to boost self-esteem,
recognize your worth and find genuine happiness*

Shainna Ali, PhD

Published by:
Ulysses Press
PO Box 3440
Berkeley, CA 94703
www.ulyssespress.com

ISBN: 978-1-61243-866-5
Library of Congress Catalog Number: 2018959575

Printed in the United States
20 19 18 17 16 15 14 13 12 11 10

Acquisitions editor: Bridget Thoreson
Managing editor: Claire Chun
Editor: Renee Rutledge
Proofreader: Shayna Keyles
Cover design: Justin Shirley
Interior design: what!design @ whatweb.com
Cover art: © Champ008/shutterstock.com
Interior art: © shutterstock.com—page 1, road © Efimova Anna; page 13, road signs © Orca; page 13, suitcase © Golden Sikorka; page 24, storm head © VectorKnight; page 29, blindspot © rumruay; page 51, glass © Aleks Melnik; page 68, toolbox © Alexander_P; page 73, cat mirror © Ken Cook; page 85, brain © Mavr88; page 108, slingshot © shockfactor.de; page 109, stopwatch © Best Vector Elements; page 115, present © koya979; page 131, hats © SofiaV
Layout: Jake Flaherty

CONTENTS

INTRODUCTION

Welcome to the beginning of a wonderful, life-changing journey! As you work through this book, you will learn to better understand, accept, and love your true self. The activities and reflection prompts included in the following pages are designed to help you increase your awareness of your own needs, desires, and dreams. By the time you reach the end of the workbook, you will come to understand the value of self-love and how to utilize it in your day-to-day life.

Please note that you may be embarking on a new, unfamiliar path. As you make your way through this book, expect to encounter helpful vehicles to support your quest but also be confronted with roadblocks that may temporarily hinder your journey. Although challenging, this expedition is paved with the promise of growth, happiness, and love. Despite the difficulties that might arise on your path to self-love, the simple act of opening this book is a huge step in the right direction! You should be proud of yourself for beginning this process. Instead of staying put in the comfortable routine of your daily life, you've chosen to honor your worth, motivation, and passion. You've chosen a personal pilgrimage to become a better version of yourself, and this dedication to discovering and loving your true self is incredibly powerful. As you work toward your personal goals, come back to this initial spark of motivation and be inspired! Although you may be fixated on the triumph at the end of the line, please remember that it is often the adventure itself that makes the biggest impact.

Before you begin, take a moment to consider how and why you have arrived at this self-love journey. Although self-love is helpful for everyone, the reasons for embracing it may vary. Delving deeper, you may find that the value of self-love changes at different phases in your life as well. The following prompts will help you to reflect on your purpose for setting out on a path paved with self-love.

As you begin with these reflections, honor what arises. Try your best to be open and nonjudgmental of your ideas and feelings. If you have been considering a question for some time, several thoughts may come to mind. On the other hand, it's quite possible that these questions may be new considerations, and you may need to be patient with yourself in the process. As you continue your journey, your reflections may become clearer with time. You are welcome to return to this reflection when the time feels right.

What has brought you to this path?

_____

_____

_____

_____

_____

_____

_____

_____

Why is this journey important to you?

_____

_____

_____

_____

_____

_____

_____

_____

What do you hope to encounter along the way?

CHAPTER 1

self-love \ , *self-luhv* \ *n.* **1.** The active practice of accepting, caring for, and encouraging oneself

Just as water and air are vital to survival, so, too, is the need to love and be loved. Is it possible that a primary part of this necessity is the ability to love oneself?

Although not a new term, the concept of self-love has been gaining popularity in recent years. Thousands are being called to consider that love is not just an interpersonal concept, feeling, or behavior but an intrapersonal process as well. We need love from ourselves as much, and perhaps more, than we do from others.

The process of self-love begins with the mere task of being able to appreciate you for you. It is crucial to be kind and considerate toward yourself; however, self-love is more than a sentiment. Beyond your ability to tend to yourself, you must remember that self-love is an intentional practice to learn and cultivate. Self-love provides you with the opportunity to see yourself completely, to recognize and value your strengths and weaknesses, triumphs and challenges. It is critical to acknowledge your imperfections and obstacles in order to nurture your personal growth.

Self-love is wondrously empowering and validating, yet it is not always an easy task. It is more than indulging in your favorite food and escaping to an island paradise. Within this process, it is helpful to recognize that without darkness there cannot be an appreciation for the light. Self-love also requires the courage to reflect on where you are, the bravery to consider where you want to be, and the tenacity to strive to be a better version of your true self.

With an emphasis on the self, this journey is ultimately an independent one. Although it is helpful to unite with others who are on a similar path, at the end of the day self-growth is predominantly dependent on personal effort. The process of loving oneself is a subjective experience. Just because a tip has worked for many does not mean it will work for all. Honor your individuality as you attempt to follow the guidance provided in this book.

While fruitful, the process of self-love is not a summit to conquer. Instead it is a continuous practice of caring for yourself. Hence, self-love includes the dedication to prioritize yourself regardless of the chaos that life may bring.

Overall, self-love is an all-encompassing practice of recognizing your self-worth, being kind toward yourself, and fostering your self-growth throughout the course of your life.

Just as the journey of self-love differs from person to person, the definition may vary as well. Take a moment to consider what self-love means to you.

_____

_____

_____

_____

_____

_____

_____

_____

THE IMPORTANCE OF SELF-LOVE

ASHA   As long as Asha can remember, she has dreamed of her prince sweeping her off of her feet in a fairy tale union. She even describes herself as the quintessential hopeless romantic on her dating profile. As she attends wedding after wedding, with a different date each time, she begins to worry. Her long list of short-term relationships has caused her to become discouraged. Asha doesn't give up. She continues to invest her all into each budding romance, only to be met with heartbreak each time. Feeling like the forever third wheel, she starts to isolate herself from her friends. When her loved ones touch base, she fears the impending awkward exchange in which she has to report time and time again that she hasn't found the one.

MARIANA   Mariana had a difficult upbringing. Born to a young mother, Mariana lived with her mother and grandmother growing up. Her mother was often out of the house and didn't spend a lot of time with her. Fortunately, Mariana had her grandmother, and eventually, younger siblings to keep her company. When Mariana was ten, her grandmother was diagnosed with stage IV cancer, which progressed quickly. The family struggled for several years to make ends meet. Mariana now feels the pressure to drop out of school to help pay the bills. Wanting a better future for herself and her family, Mariana turns to risky side jobs to juggle staying in school and helping her family.

DEVON With an empty nest and pending divorce, Devon finds himself reflecting on his life. While he spent decades establishing a notable career as a cardiothoracic surgeon, his time with his spouse and three children seems to be a blur. Although he is happy that he achieved his dream of gaining prominence in his field, he is beginning to recognize the cost of his hard work. While Devon is proud to have been able to support his family throughout the years, he is beginning to recognize that his financial support could not account for his absence. Devon becomes overwhelmed thinking about all of the moments that were missed due to his ambitious path, and how he may never have those opportunities again. Devastated, Devon turns to excessive alcohol use to numb his feelings of despair.

Now that you have a definition of self-love, consider how self-love applies to Asha, Mariana, and Devon.

What examples of self-love do you see within Asha?

_____

_____

_____

_____

_____

What examples of self-love do you see within Mariana?

_____

_____

_____

_____

_____

What examples of self-love do you see within Devon?

_____

_____

_____

_____

_____

_____

How think Asha's life may change if she improves her self-love?

_____

_____

_____

_____

_____

How do you think Mariana's life may change if she improves her self-love?

_____

_____

_____

_____

_____

_____

How do you think Devon's life may change if he improves his self-love?

_____

_____

_____

_____

_____

Asha, Mariana, and Devon are average people not too different from you. Like anyone else, th__ self-love. From these cases we catch a glimpse of a time in their lives in which they are unaware importance of self-love. At this point in time, Asha, Mariana, and Devon are all unable to see and h their worth. They do not realize that in order to care for others, we must also care for ourselves.

They have disconnected from their true selves and have been facing consequences as a result of tha severance. Asha has been focused on finding love, but in the wrong places. She has been fixated on finding someone to love her, rather than seeking to love herself first. Mariana has the best of intentions for her loved ones; however, the pressures of life have caused her to sacrifice until she is depleted and risks being unable to take care of herself or anyone else. Devon's visible successes caused him to become prideful and materialistic, and while he's excelled in his profession, he still struggles in matters of the heart.

Like anyone else, Asha, Mariana, and Devon are all capable of making the choice to infuse self-love into their lives. With that brave choice, they can explore and reconnect with their genuine selves. They can discover and embrace their strengths and embrace them to improve their quality of life. They can under-stand their areas for growth and explore them with patience and kindness. As they embrace a self-loving lifestyle they will be able to care for and respect not only themselves, but others well.

Without a strong sense of love for yourself, you may experience…

- Anxiety
- Carelessness
- Criminal behavior
- Defensiveness
- Depression
- Hopelessness
- Insecurity
- Materialism

- Negligence
- Prejudice
- Sadness
- Shame
- Stagnancy
- Suicidal thoughts
- Unhealthy coping

On the other hand, with a strong sense of love for yourself, you may benefit from gains in…

- Academic achievement
- Altruism
- Belonging
- Career success
- Confidence
- Empowerment
- Encouragement
- Enthusiasm
- Happiness

- Inspiration
- Love
- Motivation
- Passion
- Relationship quality
- Self-care
- Social support
- Physical health
- Parenting skills

WHAT SELF-LOVE ISN'T

Self-love has been met with critique. However, these appraisals are based on misunderstandings. To help clarify, let's be clear on what self-love is not.

ENTITLEMENT   When a person has a sense of entitlement, they may believe they are unconditionally owed something regardless of efforts, merit, or context. This should not be confused with the idea of recognizing your worth. Depending on your perspective on humility and deservingness, you may find it difficult to assert you are worthy of self-love. If this is the case, it may be helpful to consider basic human needs. One could argue that compassion, care, and acceptance are as fundamental as water, food, or shelter. Therefore, recognizing your worth and need for self-love overall is not that ridiculous to seek. Self-love isn't about why you deserve a billion dollars, a fancy yacht, or a mansion. It isn't an overtly ambitious jump. It isn't elite or exclusive, but a core aspect of humanity.

SELFISHNESS   Focusing on self-love is not the pathway to obsession. Although self-love is a reflective process in which one turns their energy inward, the benefits are not selfish. In actuality, in order to care for others effectively, one must first care for themselves. Prior to taking off on an airplane, the flight attendant assures flyers that in the case of an emergency, regardless of who is nearby, it is critical to first put on your oxygen mask before helping others. We wouldn't dare tell someone who abides by this regulation that they are truly selfish. Similarly, you can't pour from an empty cup. Self-focus is not egocentric; ultimately, self-focus helps you and others.

In addition, whereas narcissism may be superficial and vain, self-love is quite the opposite. Self-love delves beyond the surface and isn't all rainbows and unicorns along the way. Along with recognizing your worth, needs, and goals, self-love requires the courage to distinguish your weaknesses, challenges, and obstacles. Therefore, self-love necessitates humility, empathy, and concern for the self as well as for others.

SINFUL   A sin is an act that is not only inappropriate but often violent. Self-love is just the opposite. Self-love isn't meant to go against a principle or moral grounding; it is the enlightened journey to care for yourself in order to prompt a domino effect of care and compassion for those around you. Nevertheless, due to varying concepts of what self-love truly entails, from time to time individuals may view self-love as against their values and beliefs. Just as everyone is unique, their interpretation of scripture may vary as well. If you are struggling with differentiating self-love from sin, it may be helpful for you to research and reflect on whether or not a conflict truly exists.

Regardless of your faith or beliefs, it may be worthwhile to consider the commonalities in various world religions. Oftentimes, the tasks encapsulated with being a moral person include benevolence, forgiveness, and personal growth, all of which align well with the practice of self-love. More specifically, the golden rule of treating others as you want to be treated is the essence of self-love. From this common adage, we often jump to the lesson to treat others kindly, but we should not forget the implication requires being kind to ourselves as well.

AN EXCUSE   Self-love is an active, engaged process that evokes a wealth of positive benefits. Nevertheless, the journey is not always an easy one. A critical component in self-love is recognizing your limits, needs, and worth, and asserting intrapersonal and interpersonal boundaries as needed to uphold them. While this all-encompassing process may include mental health days, massages, and indulging in your favorite home-cooked meal, it is not an exploitation of all things good. Ironically, perpetual pampering could actually be neglectful and, hence, distinct from self-love. The full process of self-love includes the good, the bad, and the ugly. Beyond the stereotypically positive perks, self-love also includes the decision to recognize your areas for growth, tailoring a potentially difficult yet necessary plan of attack, and bravely tackling it head on. To an outsider without context, self-love could appear as an excuse; however, it is critical that you not use self-love as your hall pass to escape responsibility, accountability, and difficult situations in general. In contrast, true self-love can be enacted by taking accountability and responsibility as you courageously embark on arduous paths.

"Love yourself first and everything else falls into line. You really have to love yourself to get anything done in this world."
—Lucille Ball

OBSTACLES IN SELF-LOVE

*"Your task is not to seek for love, but merely to seek and find all
the barriers within yourself that you have built against it."*

—Rumi

Recognizing what is holding you back from loving yourself and living a happier, healthier life is a crucial component as you prepare to tackle these challenges on your path to self-love. Since self-love is a subjective journey, the obstacles may vary from person to person. Our unique combination of attributes, such as our history, intentions, beliefs, personality, values, and goals, may coalesce and connect us to the self-love process. However, these characteristics may combine to create roadblocks as well. Although variation is expected, there are some common concerns that impede on the ability to love oneself.

ABUSE Physical, sexual, and psychological abuse all provoke consequences that may risk severe impairment. Individuals who endure abuse often have feelings of shame and guilt that inhibit their ability to seek help and heal. Even past memories of abuse can be pervasive and may be triggered, thus distracting from and impeding one's progress in the present.

Abuse often happens at the hands of someone who is known and trusted. This person could be a loved one, such as a parent or partner. This betrayal can foster a lack of trust in oneself and in others, causing one to question their worth and encounter issues with self-esteem, self-confidence, and self-respect. All forms of abuse may yield psychological consequences. Psychological abuse includes pain without overt physical harm, which may cause the severity of psychological concerns to be further ignored, minimized, or difficult to recognize. Sticks, stones, and words can be painful. Name-calling, yelling, insulting, threatening, excluding, mocking, humiliating, and criticizing all have the potential to be deeply painful and powerful offenses that often prohibit a person's ability to love themselves.

COMPARISONS One of the ways we tend to harm ourselves is by drawing comparisons. They may arise out of an innocent observation, and could even be motivational. However, when comparisons morph into pure negativity, they have the potential to form large roadblocks in your journey of self-love. Comparisons become a grave concern when they are habitual, obsessive, and/or constant. It is one thing to utilize a comparison to inform your assessment of your progress, but when exploited, this previously useful tactic feeds your inner self-critic. As negative self-talk increases and loudens, the inner encourager may weaken and fade into the background. Over time, what may have been a seemingly innocuous analysis can carve out an unrealistic, impossible standard paired with a self-defeating mindset that suppresses the ability to love yourself.

MENTAL ILLNESS Tending to proper mental health care is fundamental to a successful journey of self-love. While all individuals can benefit from self-love in their lives, loving oneself is not the solution to mental illness. Self-love can certainly be helpful for those who live with mental health diagnoses, especially those pertaining to anxiety, depression, interpersonal problems, and trauma; nevertheless, it is not an appropriate replacement for professional mental health care. Furthermore, consistent setbacks on the path of self-love may point to an unattended mental health concern. If this occurs, it is important to consult with a mental health professional to assist you in shedding light on previously unidentified concerns. Bringing awareness to a prior hidden concern may be an empowering shift in your process. Equipped with a qualified clinician and your will to set out on your self-love journey, you can cross over the hurdle of illness impeding your ultimate success.

DANGER Existential psychologist Abraham Maslow asserted that humans have five basic levels of needs: physiological, safety, social, esteem, and self-actualization. The hierarchy of needs conveys that the primary needs are sequential in nature. All individuals are capable of arriving at the pinnacle, self-actualization. After a process of surpassing requisite needs, an individual enjoys a sense of genuine fulfillment. To achieve improvements in self-esteem, self-growth, and self-love, you must first establish foundational needs—physiological, safety, and social. Although self-love is a necessity, it is important to recognize priorities. An unwillingness to consider a hierarchy could cause you to become frustrated by placing your energy on self-love when it is not presently possible to be absorbed within that domain. You wouldn't enroll in calculus without rudimentary mathematic knowledge, and you should approach your needs similarly.

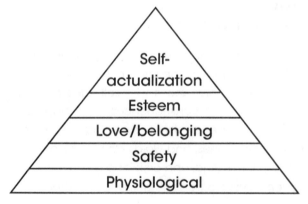

Maslow's hierarchy of needs

For individuals who are struggling to put food on the table or even find shelter (physiological and safety needs), the ability to focus on self-love is not unneeded, it may simply be a luxury within that context. If a challenging phase in life shakes your foundation, it is certainly justified if you choose to temporarily pause your current self-love to regain your equilibrium.

In reference to the social domain, we need others just as they may need us. When our loved ones need our attention, care, and love, it is understandable to deter from our journey to help them. Our esteem needs encompass how we view ourselves and how others view us as well. While we may often rely on others to serve as a mirror for our esteem, it is important to remember that self-esteem is fostered internally. Therefore, fulfilling our esteem needs are a balance of our views and those of others. Regardless of the level, our needs may be tested throughout our lives, and it is helpful to remember to tend to our fundamentals so we can continue on our self-love journey.

ROADBLOCKS TO SELF-LOVE

While on the journey of self-love, roadblocks are to be expected. Noting the common obstacles mentioned on the previous pages, take a moment to consider the unique hurdles that may stall your individual progress.

_____

_____

_____

_____

_____

_____

PREPARING FOR YOUR JOURNEY

This workbook will likely be easy to read, but harder to practice. Unfortunately, simply reading the material will not improve your self-love. To fully engage in this journey, you will need to be open and honest with yourself. There may be moments in which you feel the need to detour from unfamiliar territory. When you encounter areas you are not yet ready to delve deep into, a detour may be helpful. As you continue in your journey, you may gain the tools needed to return to and tackle these obstacles. However, making this a habit and consistently veering around essential points in the process may inhibit your growth.

You can skim through the pages of this workbook quite quickly, but processing and applying the core concepts will take more time. This journey will require patience. If you were preparing for a marathon, you would not expect yourself to run 26.2 miles on the first day of training. Chances are that you would not view this as a defeat. Instead, you would intentionally condition yourself for the challenge by allocating the necessary time, energy, and preparations. Furthermore, you would be kind and encouraging to yourself as you strove to reach your goal.

Although there can be interpersonal aspects and benefits of self-love, it is predominately an intrapersonal process, responsibility, and commitment. There will certainly be peaks in which you will recognize your growth, and valleys consisting of more difficult moments. Therefore, this process requires courage as you anticipate both wonderful achievements and trying tasks. Your unique, reflective, and engaging journey to improve your overall practice of self-love will persist beyond this workbook as true self-love is a continuous process rather than a destination.

What do you need to prepare prior to embarking on this journey?

_____

_____

_____

_____

_____

_____

SEVEN SEGMENTS OF SELF-LOVE

In the chapters that follow you will travel through the seven segments of self-love. Before you delve into deeper reflection, take a moment to consider where you believe you are in each:

1. Self-awareness is the ability to recognize who you are, how you influence the world, and how the world influences you. Self-awareness encompasses your ability to attune to and take accountability for your thoughts, feelings, and behaviors.

2. Self-exploration is the courage to delve into learning about yourself in order to improve your knowledge of who you are.

3. Self-care is comprised of a wide variety of tasks that require you to take care of your overall wellness.

4. Self-esteem is the result of how you view your overall self.

5. Self-kindness is the skill of being friendly to yourself.

6. Self-respect is the empowered ability to advocate for oneself.

7. Self-growth is the continual process of seeking opportunities to learn, love, and thrive.

Gauge your present status in each of the seven areas and share below.

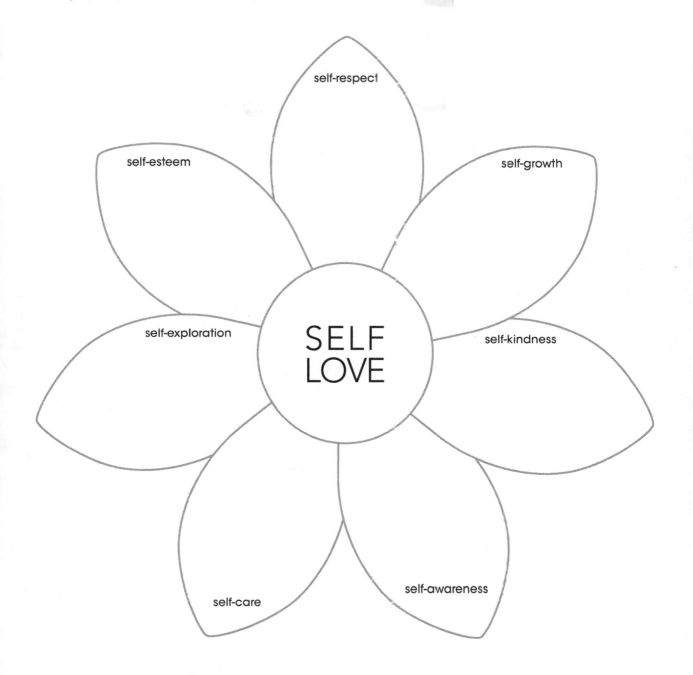

CHAPTER 2

SELF-AWARENESS

Through introspection, you are better able to understand your thoughts, feelings, desires, motives, and overall self. In this process you attune to your experiences through intentional and judgment-free observation. Your reflection equips you with the ability to promote your well-being by being conscientious and engaged. Self-awareness allows you to recognize when you are in need of self-love and when you are actively fostering your self-love. Without this recognition you could find yourself lost on your self-love journey.

Whether open-ended or prompted, journaling is a helpful tool for tuning into your awareness, connecting you to your inner world, and reflecting at any stage in your self-love journey. Writing will be encouraged throughout this book as a way for you to recognize your views and reactions on a deeper level.

Let's try an open-ended reflection on your self-awareness.

Explore your thoughts, feelings, and desires in this very moment.

EMOTIONAL EXPLORATION

*"Be who you are and say what you feel, because those who
mind don't matter and those who matter don't mind."*

—Dr. Seuss

Being able to recognize your emotions, or how you are feeling in any given moment, is a strength and a key part of self-awareness. For example, if you can pinpoint when you feel overwhelmed, you can be empowered to tend to your self-care. The inability to be cognizant of your feelings inhibits your capacity to understand and love yourself. Here are 100 feeling words to help you explore your emotional experiences in the activities provided throughout this workbook.

100 Feeling Words

Agitated	Chipper	Encouraged	Humiliated
Alert	Committed	Enraged	Inadequate
Alienated	Compassionate	Enthusiastic	Independent
Amazed	Concerned	Excited	Inferior
Angry	Confident	Fearful	Infuriated
Annoyed	Confused	Focused	Insecure
Apathetic	Content	Fortunate	Inspired
Appalled	Creative	Frustrated	Intrigued
Appreciated	Curious	Furious	Irate
Apprehensive	Dedicated	Grateful	Irritated
Astonished	Defensive	Happy	Joyful
Awed	Dejected	Heartbroken	Listless
Betrayed	Disappointed	Honored	Lonely
Bored	Disgusted	Hopeful	Loving
Calm	Eager	Hopeless	Mad
Caring	Embarrassed	Horrified	Miserable

Motivated	Playful	Scared	Tired
Neglected	Powerful	Sensitive	Trustful
Nervous	Productive	Serene	Uninterested
Offended	Proud	Shocked	Unworthy
Optimistic	Rejected	Stressed	Vigilant
Ostracized	Remorseful	Submissive	Vulnerable
Passive	Resentful	Sullen	Weak
Peaceful	Sad	Thoughtful	Withdrawn
Perplexed	Safe	Threatened	Worried

EMOTIONAL AWARENESS

Take a moment to tune into your emotions. In this very instant, how do you feel?

In this moment I feel...

_____

_____

_____

_____

_____

_____

_____

_____

_____

Delve deeper—are you aware of why you feel the way you do?

For example: I feel <u>excited</u> because <u>I am learning how to improve my self-love</u>.

I feel _____ because _____

_____

I feel _____ because _____

_____

EMOTIONAL EQUATIONS

When reflecting on your feelings, you may have noticed that you can experience a combination of emotions at once. That is perfectly fine.

Reflect on how you feel with the following combinations of emotions, or emotional equations, to foster your self-awareness.

Relaxed + Creative =

_____

Happy + Sad =

_____

Excited + Confident =

_____

Lonely + Insecure =

_____

Inadequate + Foolish =

_____

Playful + Cheerful =

_____

Important + Thankful =

_____

It is common to experience multiple emotions in a given situation. Recognizing that you are likely to have more than one feeling at a time helps you to broaden your awareness in a given situation. If you found it easy to think of times in which you experienced the combinations described, that may signal a strong emotional awareness. Continue to consider combinations to illuminate your emotional experiences and improve your self-awareness.

If it was difficult for you, that's okay. Be patient with yourself. Now that you better understand that feelings can be complex depending on context, you will be able to practice refining your awareness in the present. Feel free to return to these reflections to continue to foster your emotional awareness.

THE DEPTH OF EMOTIONS

Knowing what prompts your emotions is another self-awareness skill that helps you to better understand yourself and the world around you.

Let's explore your self-awareness. For each emotion below, consider how you are before and after the emotion. Consider what triggers you to feel that emotion and what is the effect of that feeling. Triggers and effects can be thoughts, feelings, or behaviors. They can include other people as well. You can use general examples that are common to you or specific memories from the past.

Example from Sam:

When...
I'm alone

I feel...
bored

and then...
I tend to binge watch TV

In the example on above, Sam recognized a habit in which she was watching too much TV. Although TV tends to help Sam de-stress, she has recognized that she often loses track of time and feels drained when watching too much TV. When reflecting on how emotions may play into this situation, Sam realizes that she tends to turn to TV when she is bored. Being unoccupied and underwhelmed makes it easy for her to watch episode after episode. Although watching TV fills up her time, Sam wants to use her free time for other hobbies, such as crafting and exercising. Recognizing this connection, Sam has heightened her awareness to turn first to her hobbies instead of TV when she feels bored.

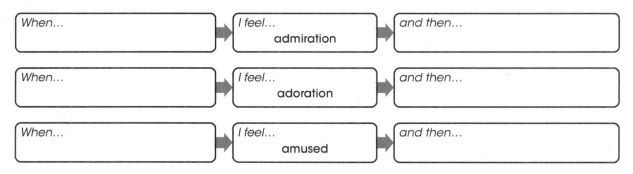

When...

I feel...
admiration

and then...

When...

I feel...
adoration

and then...

When...

I feel...
amused

and then...

When...	I feel... anxious	and then...
When...	I feel... awkward	and then...
When...	I feel... bored	and then...
When...	I feel... calm	and then...
When...	I feel... confused	and then...
When...	I feel... disgusted	and then...
When...	I feel... entranced	and then...
When...	I feel... envious	and then...
When...	I feel... excited	and then...
When...	I feel... fearful	and then...
When...	I feel... horrified	and then...
When...	I feel... joyful	and then...
When...	I feel... nostalgic	and then...
When...	I feel... romantic	and then...

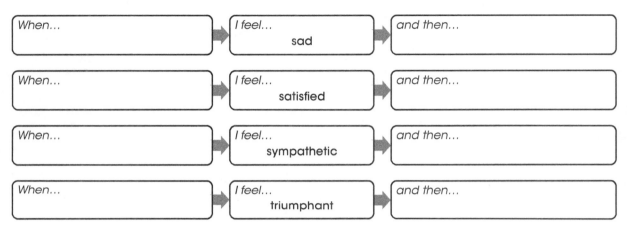

When…	I feel… sad	and then…
When…	I feel… satisfied	and then…
When…	I feel… sympathetic	and then…
When…	I feel… triumphant	and then…

The ability to understand feelings is an attribute of emotional intelligence. You were able to practice two aspects of understanding: the root and the effect. The root is what may underlie an emotion whereas the effect occurs as a result of the emotion arising. These reflections allow you to consider the depth of your emotional experience and to begin to understand how your feelings may affect your thoughts and behaviors.

MINDFULNESS

In our world it is easy to be distracted and often difficult to be present. This reality often blocks our self-awareness. If you are submerged in the chaos of the noise around you, tuning into yourself can be a challenging endeavor. The ancient practice of mindfulness can be a helpful tool to overcome this common hurdle and to improve your self-awareness.

The evolution of thousands of years of mindfulness practice spanning across the globe can be interpreted differently from person to person. For the self-awareness purpose of this workbook, we will recognize mindfulness as a sincere state of presence in which you are conscientious, attentive, and engaged. When you are mindful you are not consumed by what has happened or what is to come. Instead you are actively involved in the here and now. Additionally, you are a calm and kind observer who is immersed in the experience and is not inundated by judgments.

While mindfulness is a process, several activities noted on the next two pages work to engage mindfulness. Benefits of mindful practice include improvements in memory, sense of self, empathy, and decision making, and reductions in worries, stress, poor coping, and perceptions of chronic pain. Although mindfulness may seem simple, small adjustments have been shown to make a substantial impact. Mindfulness methods have been powerful enough to reduce symptoms of post-traumatic stress disorder in veterans and symptoms of distress in cancer patients.

Mindfulness does not fit into the stereotype of seated and stationary meditation. Hence, you can practice mindfulness when talking, eating, and walking. When you are mindful, you are engaged and nonjudgmentally observant in the present moment To be mindful, you play an observer in your own life. If you attune your awareness in a given moment and rid yourself of criticism, you are practicing the essence of mindfulness.

Taking this a step further, mindfulness can be used to foster your self-loving practice. Here are three ways to use mindfulness to hone your self-awareness:

Breathing: Take note of your breathing. Recognize where the breath enters the body. Note where the breath leaves the body. Begin to slow your breath. As you continue, notice how the breath affects your body. Pay attention to the subtle movement that each breath brings to the body, with every inhale and every exhale. Place one hand on your chest as you continue to breathe. Notice the sensation of the lungs filling with air and decompressing with each exhale. Inhale as you slowly count 1-2-3. Pause. Exhale as you count 3-2-1. Continue as needed.

Body scan: Find a comfortable seated position. Soften your gaze. Notice your body. Recognize your posture. Note how your body connects to the seat. Now, bring your awareness to your breath. Slowly inhale and slowly exhale. Begin to elongate your exhales, making them longer than your inhales.

Continue to breathe as you bring your awareness to your feet. Notice any tension that you may have in the bottoms of your feet, your ankles, or toes. Take a deep inhale, and on a slow exhale try to relax your feet.

Continue to breathe as you bring your awareness to your knees. Notice any tension that you may have in your knees, shins, or calves. Take a deep inhale, and with your next exhale try to release this tension.

As your awareness moves up the legs, notice any tension that you may be holding in your thighs, pelvis, or glutes. Inhale, and release this tension as you exhale. Bring your attention up to your midsection, then up to your chest. As you inhale, note any tension in these areas and release with your elongated exhale.

Bring your attention to your shoulders through the tips of your fingers. Recognize the tension that may be in your arms with your inhale, and release that tension with your exhale.

Finally, notice any tension from your neck to the crown of your head. Take the longest inhale of this practice, and release any tension from the crown of your head to the base of your feet with the longest exhale of this practice. Using this elongated breath, on the next inhale squeeze every inch of your body tight. Curl the toes, create fists, squeeze your glutes, and tighten your face. On the next elongated exhale release this tremendous tension, allowing your body to sink and relax. Continue to breathe as needed.

Cloud watching: Mental noise can distract us from our ability to be mindful and self-aware. One thought often breeds another thought. In this activity, focus on acknowledging your thoughts but allowing yourself to be released of them as well. Expend your energy on observing rather than questioning or avoiding your thoughts. Imagine that you are lying in a lush green field, looking up at the clouds moving across the sky. As they scroll from left to right, you observe them and let them pass. Imagine each of your thoughts is attached to a single cloud. Recognize each thought as it enters your scope and allow it to pass with the subtle rotation of the earth.

These three activities will help you to train your mindfulness muscle. They may seem simple, but the practices may be quite difficult. Use them as a challenge to become more mindful. Try to be patient with yourself.

We all experience storm clouds that affect us as they pass by. These clouds are thoughts that inhibit our presence, engagement, and nonjudgmental positioning. Although the storm clouds are a subjective experience, they often consist of thoughts that are difficult to let go of, future tasks, or random distractions. A key in self-awareness is recognizing where difficulties exist. As you continue to practice mindfulness, notice your storm clouds.

SELF-KNOWLEDGE

"We don't see things as they are, we see them as we are."

—Anaïs Nin

Attuning to your personal awareness allows you to know yourself better. Self-awareness can include fleeting moments, but can also encompass deeper and consistent pieces of who you are. Self-awareness is a requisite for the recognition and reflection that equate to self-knowledge. Knowing yourself is essential to understanding what self-love means specifically to you. It helps you to better understand, and differentiate from, others as well. When you begin to use your awareness to hone your self-knowledge, your reflection can allow you to see strengths and capabilities you may not have previously recognized. Connecting to self-knowledge allows you to consider what contributes to your self-love, what inhibits your self-love, and what you require in your self-love journey.

Use the categories below to delve into what you know about you.

I am	I have	I love

My strengths	My pet peeves	I aspire to

CULTURAL EXPLORATION

"A mind cannot be independent of culture."
—Lev Vygotsky

One way to strengthen your self-knowledge is to reflect on the depth of your culture. Oftentimes we may limit our view of culture by a common variable such as race or gender; however, culture is much more. Although you may have similarities to those in your family, community, or country, your cultural composition is unique to you. Your culture can span to include a variety of domains. Within each of these areas, culture encompasses your customs, values, beliefs, and traditions. Pamela Hays's ADDRESSING framework was created to help highlight various cultural domains and how they may interact.

Take a moment to reflect on your identity for each segment.

Age/Generation _____

Disability Status (Congenital) _____

Disability Status (Acquired) _____

Religion/Spiritual Orientation _____

Socioeconomic Status _____

Sexual Orientation _____

Indigenous Heritage _____

National Origin _____

Gender _____

Cultural domains are vast and include where you are from the groups you belong to, the social roles that you fulfill, and the activities that you like to do. Some of these aspects of your culture may be encapsulated in the model above. Although these are common cultural realms, it is not an exhaustive list. Culture varies from person to person.

What are some of the additional domains of your culture?

_____

_____

_____

_____

1. Consider the vast variables of cultural self-knowledge noted on the previous page. Take a moment and choose four of your cultural domains.

2. Reflect on what each piece means to you. How does each domain affect who you are?

3. For each domain, consider if there are aspects of this identity variable that may help your ability to provide yourself with love.

4. For each domain, consider if there are aspects of this identity variable that may inhibit your ability to provide yourself with love.

5. Finally, reflect on how each piece may warrant a different type of self-love.

Example:

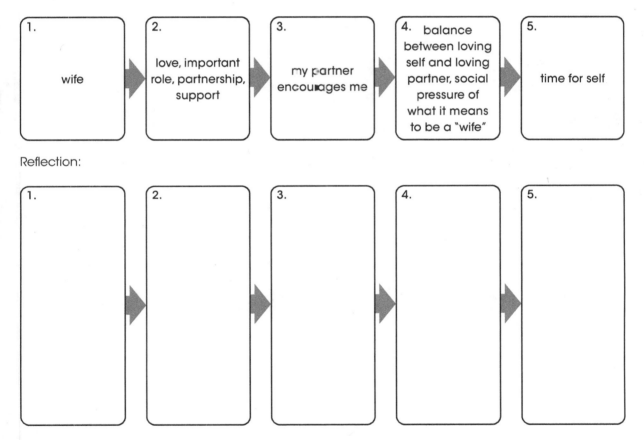

Reflection:

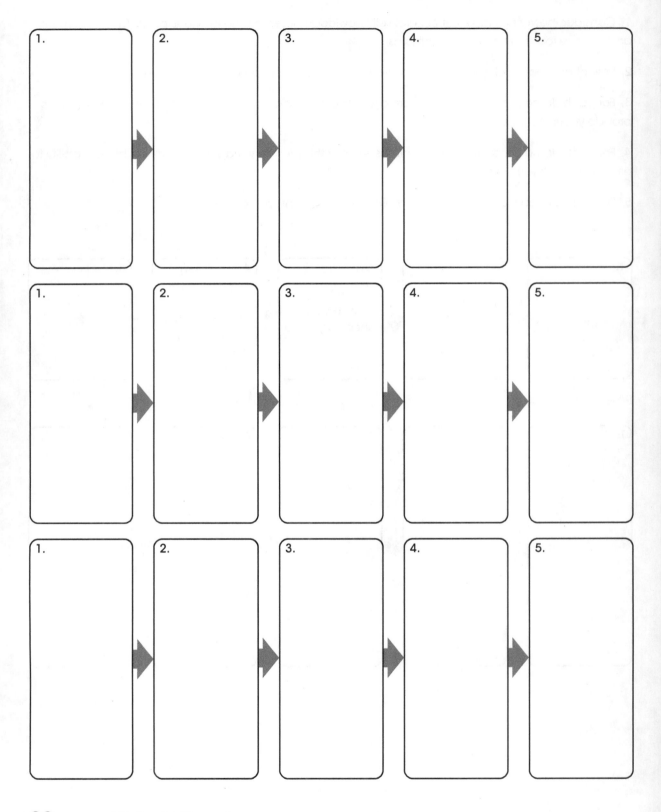

the SELF-LOVE WORKBOOK

HIGHLIGHTING STRENGTHS

As you prepared for your self-love journey, you considered the roadblocks that you may encounter along the way (see activity Roadblocks to Self-Love on page 13). While practicing self-love, you may learn that your strengths can help you to endure difficult terrain. If you take the time to bring your strengths into your awareness you will be able to use them in a time of need. The ability to connect to positivity during a challenging moment may help to support, protect, and foster your resilience.

What provides you with the momentum to propel forward on your self-love path?

_____

_____

_____

_____

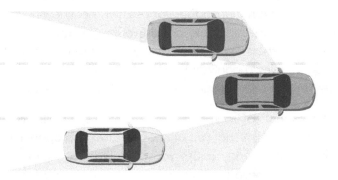

FINDING BLIND SPOTS

"Sometimes you can't see yourself clearly until you
see yourself through the eyes of others."
—Ellen DeGeneres

Heightening self-awareness and improving self-knowledge is ongoing within your self-love journey. Regardless of your effort and intention along this path, it is normal to have blind spots. Our knowledge of ourselves, and how others view us, can be distorted and difficult to see. Self-distancing can allow you to step back and reflect on your blind spots. However, even then, your periphery may be limited. With an awareness of this limitation, you can seek help from others to illuminate your blind spots and improve your self-knowledge.

The Johari Window was created by psychologists Joseph Luft and Harrington Ingham as a method to help enhance self-awareness and promote personal development. It can be used to help you to reflect on what is within and beyond your current self-knowledge. Each of the four quadrants define a different aspect of knowledge that ranges from what you know about yourself to what others may know about you. Those quadrants are the arena, the façade, the blind spot, and the unknown area.

The arena can be thought of as a public space. In this area, you would list characteristics that are openly known both to yourself and others. Visible characteristics may fall into this domain; however, clearly observable traits may be included as well. Imagine that you have just moved to a new town and you have been invited to your first dinner party. Excited to make connections in your new location, you are eager to meet each guest. Even to those who are still distant affiliations, your enthusiasm is clear from your smiling face.

The façade, on the other hand, is a domain in which you may have awareness about a personal characteristic that others do not. For example, acquaintances may not know nuanced aspects of your identity, such as whether or not you are charitable or trustworthy. This quadrant includes characteristics you may intentionally hide from others. For example, when meeting your partner's parents for the first time, you may be nervous but convey a confident and self-assured demeanor instead. If you are successful in minimizing your true sentiments, your suppression qualifies your nervousness to be within the façade.

The blind spot includes aspects of yourself that others may see while your own perspective could be lacking. For example, you may think that you are cooperative and open-minded; however, a brainstorming session with your colleagues may cause you to realize that your efforts in collaboration may be interpreted in another way. At these sessions, you may sit back and listen to be polite and receptive, whereas your peers may value hearing your opinions and unique perspectives.

The unknown area includes aspects of yourself that you and others do not know. This may include knowledge that is beyond your realm, such as future predictions. However, the unknown quadrant can also include information that simply lies beyond awareness. For example, you may notice that you tend to gravitate to toxic relationships. What may be unknown to you and others is that you may be influenced by the relationships that were modeled to you by your family as you were growing up.

Fill in the Johari Window on the next page. You may opt to leave areas you do not know blank. However, you could reflect on details not previously known that became illuminated with the help of others. You may also choose to reflect on what you would like to learn to fill these areas. The Room for Growth list (page 106) may be useful to you to draw on here.

Johari Window

	Known to self	Not known to self
Known to others	Arena	Blind spot
Not known to others	Facace	Unknown

Can you think of a time that something was in your blind spot, hence inhibiting your self-awareness, self-knowledge, and self-love?

_____

_____

_____

_____

_____

_____

FEEDBACK

Feedback from a trusted source, such as a good friend or positive mentor, can help you to see what may exist in your blind spots. Genuine feedback is constructive, caring, and propelled by the opportunity for growth.

Can you think of a time when someone may have tried to provide you with feedback to shed light on your blind spot?

_____

_____

_____

_____

_____

_____

_____

Were you able to receive this feedback?

_____

_____

_____

_____

_____

_____

_____

How can you be open to feedback in the future?

Being open to feedback in your journey can help you to grow. As you develop your own view, you can still benefit from the perspectives of others. You may opt to integrate their feedback, or you may self-reflect and choose to respect but set aside that feedback as well. As a continuous process, feedback can be useful in refining your growth process.

Imagine you are learning to play a guitar for the first time. You have decided to take lessons from a skilled player to help you. As you learn, the feedback from your teacher helps you to tweak your skills and enhance your abilities. You receive the feedback and can tell your playing has improved. Your progress makes you feel confident in your abilities to learn. Your instructor validates your advancement and provides you with feedback to challenge your new level of skill. In this process, the feedback is not because you are a terrible player. The feedback is used to point you in the direction of achieving your goal.

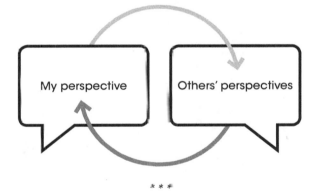

* * *

Self-awareness is an important factor in self-love. Practicing self-awareness and introspection helps you to better understand and connect with yourself. In this chapter you were able to delve into different aspects of your awareness, from your emotions to your overall identity. Reflection allows you to recognize and respect parts of yourself that you may have otherwise ignored. Additionally, practicing self-awareness signals you to pieces of you that are in need.

CHAPTER 3

SELF-EXPLORATION

"Who looks outside, dreams; who looks inside, awakes."

—Carl Jung

Self-exploration is the courage to learn about yourself to improve your knowledge of who you are. Self-knowledge begins in awareness and develops through the process of self-exploration, as you consider what you know about yourself and continue to explore depths that you may not always connect to, but need to understand in order to love yourself. Without self-exploration you may be ignorant to crucial components of who you are, such as your identity, values, and purpose. Since you are continually evolving as a human being, without self-exploration, you may risk becoming stagnant in your self-love journey.

Your self-exploration path may include twists and turns. You may encounter pieces of you that were previously unknown, as well as other pieces you have only seen glimpses of in the past. Finally, you may be able to anticipate what you will encounter due to a heightened sense of self-awareness. Whatever the case, what may be different this time is the willingness to pursue, rather than to avoid, your exploratory path.

What do you anticipate you will encounter in your self-exploration?

_____

_____

_____

_____

_____

GETTING TO KNOW YOU

Take some time to get to know you. Ask yourself the following questions in order to delve a bit deeper into your self-learning process.

What is my favorite color?

_____

What is my favorite band?

_____

Who is my favorite artist?

_____

What is my favorite book?

_____

What is my favorite movie?

_____

What is my favorite food?

_____

What is my favorite animal?

_____

What do I like to do for fun?

_____

_____

If I had only one wish, what would it be?

_____

_____

What is my proudest accomplishment?

_____

_____

What are my strengths?

_____

_____

Who do I love?

_____

_____

What new activities am I interested in or willing to try?

_____

_____

What am I ashamed of?

_____

_____

What am I worried about?

_____

_____

Where do I feel safest?

_____

_____

If I wasn't afraid I would...

_____

_____

What do I like about my job?

_____

_____

What does my inner critic tell me?

_____

_____

When I'm feeling down I like to...

_____

_____

I know I'm stressed when...

_____

_____

What do I do to show self-love?

_____

_____

What is my happiest memory?

_____

_____

What am I passionate about?

_____

_____

What am I grateful for?

_____

_____

Did some additional questions pop up? Share them and the answers here!

_____

_____

_____

THE INDEPENDENT INTERVIEW

Self-exploration is a continuous process in which the effort to better understand your true self is persistent and consistent. This process is prompted in moments in which your self-awareness recognizes the need to discover a deeper depth. Your self-awareness can be triggered by external events (e.g., conversations with others, current events); however, the impetus to look within must come from you.

The prompts on the previous page helped you to begin your self-exploration. Now, try to practice self-exploration with both questions and answers that come directly from you, in any domain you like. Choose whatever topic comes to mind, allowing new questions to come up without judgment.

QUESTIONS	ANSWERS

MY STORY

Knowing your narrative can illuminate the history that has shaped who you are today.

Use the prompts below to detail your narrative.

When I was born...

_____

_____

_____

_____

As a child I enjoyed...

_____

_____

_____

_____

Some of my challenges included...

_____

_____

_____

_____

My favorite memory is...

_____

_____

_____

_____

I faced obstacles along my path that...

_____

_____

_____

_____

I was able to grow by...

_____

_____

_____

_____

I've learned...

_____

_____

_____

_____

Use this space to share additional important chapters that may not have been encapsulated above.

_____

_____

_____

_____

_____

_____

_____

Since self-exploration is an ongoing process, your narrative is bound to continue. Use the prompts on this page to explore your future story.

What do I hope to learn in the future?

_____

_____

_____

_____

What do I hope to experience in the future?

_____

_____

_____

_____

What do I hope to happen in the future?

_____

_____

_____

_____

MY MISSION STATEMENT

"Those who have a why to live can bear with almost any how."
—Nietzsche

Reflecting on your narrative helps you better understand who you are and allows you to live a connected and loving life. Considering how far you have come lays the foundation for you to think about the second half of your story, your personal mission. Adding onto your hopes for your future, take a moment to consider your purpose. Your mission statement allows you to thread together the past and future by connecting deeply to your identity.

Here are prompts to assist you in exploring your personal purpose. Use the lines on this page to brainstorm and create your mission statement.

- What is your life's purpose?

- What is your calling?

- When do you feel most fulfilled?

- What contributes to your overall well-being?

- What do you want to accomplish?

- How do you want to live your life?

- What makes you happiest?

- What moments have felt the most purposeful?

- How do you want to be remembered?

_____

_____

_____

_____

_____

_____

_____

_____

_____

_____

CULTURAL EXPLORATION

*"Our diversity is our strength. What a dull and pointless
life it would be if everyone was the same."*
—Angelina Jolie

In Chapter 2, you had an opportunity to begin to heighten your awareness of aspects of your culture and how they may affect your self-love. Now, you will delve further into understanding the complexity of your culture in order to better understand who you are.

Previously you selected four domains. You may use those; however, challenge yourself to see the various aspects of who you are. Remember, components of your culture may include elements such as age, ethnicity, socioeconomic status, sexual orientation, gender, nationality, heritage, ability level, relationship status, social roles, education, career, and hobbies.

Brainstorm the components of your culture, then select eight of these components for the activity on the opposite page.

_____

_____

_____

_____

_____

_____

_____

_____

_____

_____

_____

INTERSECTING IDENTITIES

Oftentimes, we consider the aspects of our culture independently. However, culture is complex. Our identities are better understood by exploring how the different pieces of ourselves intersect and interact.

Place the labels in the corresponding circles. For each intersection, consider what this convergence means for you. For example, what does it mean to be a young parent? What does it mean to be Asian and American? What does it mean to be bisexual and male?

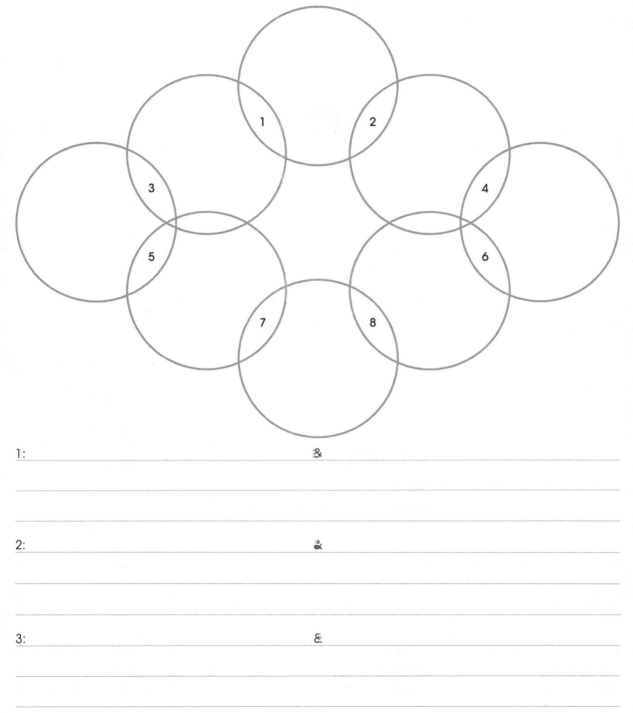

1: _____ & _____

_____

_____

2: _____ & _____

_____

_____

3: _____ & _____

_____

_____

4: _____ & _____

5: _____ & _____

6: _____ & _____

7: _____ & _____

8: _____ & _____

INNER CONFLICT

*"Happiness is when what you think, what you say,
and what you do are in harmony."*
—Mahatma Gandhi

By this point you may have learned a bit more about who you are. Nothing may be entirely new, but the way you are reflecting may be. You may have encountered pieces of yourself that are consistent in theme, but it is also possible that this exploration may have highlighted ways in which there may be inner conflict.

In order to give yourself the love you deserve, you must first recognize when there is dissonance within you. This may take the form of discordant thoughts, feelings, beliefs, values, experiences, and behaviors. As two like magnets, these forces may repel and cause you unhappiness. You must then work toward reducing the tension. You have the power to foster internal congruence and to live a life in which your thoughts, feelings, beliefs, values, experiences, and behaviors align.

Examples:

You value honesty and trust, but are cheating on your partner.

You feel hurt when people say negative things behind your back, but you continue to gossip with others.

You want to buy a house, but you carelessly spend your paychecks.

EXPLORING INNER CONFLICT

Take a moment to consider an inner conflict you may have. Place the contrasting factors in the opposing boxes below.

When you excavate an inner conflict there are three points to consider:

1. Where does this conflict arise from?

_____

_____

2. How does this conflict affect me?

_____

_____

3. How can I take charge to achieve congruence?

_____

_____

CREATIVE EXPLORATION

You have delved into the depths of your true self, excavated potential conflicts, and addressed how to achieve alignment. Self-exploration can be a mentally and emotionally draining process of discovery. However, it is a critical process in understanding how to better love yourself. When you take part in potentially arduous reflections, it's essential to check in with yourself and take care of yourself.

As you prepare to learn about self-care, tie the elements of self-learning and self-nurturing together by considering metaphors that define you. Embrace your creativity and use the space below to write, draw, or doodle.

* * *

In order to know how to love yourself, you must know yourself. Delving deep into your identity requires courage. In this chapter you bravely explored your narrative in the past, present, and future. You were able to connect to who you are and the life you wish to live.

SELF-EXPLORATION REFLECTION

CHAPTER 4

SELF-CARE

*"There is only one corner of the universe you can be
certain of improving, and that's your own self."*
—Aldous Huxley

Self-care is a holistic process that we all need in order to foster presence, engagement, wellness, and self-love. Self-care is not a singular skill. Instead, self-care includes a wide variety of tasks tailored to meet your diverse needs. Although there may be similarities between self-care strategies, self-care is subjective and tends to vary from person to person. Common dimensions of self-care include physical, creative, spiritual, natural, social, and personal. Examples of self-care activities include getting adequate sleep, practicing mindfulness, taking part in hobbies, and meditation.

Oftentimes, self-care is easier said than done. Nevertheless, it is important to give yourself the ability to reflect on and tend to your wellness. Neglecting your personal needs can cause you to suffer from deterioration in wellness and self-love. For example, you may notice increases in anxiety, distractibility, anger, and fatigue. You may also experience decreases in sleep, relationship satisfaction, self-esteem, empathy, and compassion. Ongoing exposure to stress without proper self-care can put you at risk for serious consequences such as depression and heart disease.

Therefore, self-care is a continuous process of proactively considering and tending to your needs and maintaining your wellness. As a preventative measure, self-care helps you to consider and implement strategies prior to being faced with challenges. As a coping skill, self-care helps you to recognize when a new need calls for your attention. As an ongoing process, self-care helps you to develop resilience and compassion for yourself in your overall journey of self-love.

Self-care can be tricky. It is easy to forget to take care of yourself, particularly before your loved ones. When you are low on energy and short on time, you may be especially likely to give up your own needs for the sake of someone else. Over time this can be dangerous. Also, when caring for others, it is helpful to demonstrate the importance of taking care of yourself to set an example and deter them from self-neglect as well.

If someone you know is stranded on the side of the road because their car ran out of gas, do you empty your gas tank for them? Instead, you would likely use what you have to help that person get gas for their tank. Although kind, giving up all of your gas to help someone else creates a new problem altogether. The more effective way would be to fill your tank so you can better help someone fill theirs.

FILL YOUR CUP

How do you fill your self-care cup? Provide three examples below.

1. _____

_____

2. _____

_____

3. _____

_____

Let's take this a little deeper. Why do you turn to these methods?

1. _____

_____

2. _____

_____

3. _____

_____

When you follow through with these examples, how do you feel?

_____

_____

_____

_____

_____

_____

_____

When you lack the time or energy to follow through with these examples, do you notice a difference?

_____

_____

_____

_____

_____

_____

_____

_____

YOUR WELLNESS

To expand your self-care strategies, it will be helpful to take a step back and understand your overall wellness. Wellness is a multidimensional concept of health. Self-care encompasses the methods that you utilize to support and maintain your wellness. The definition of wellness may vary from person to person. Just as self-care is subjective, wellness is often subjective as well.

How do you define wellness?

_____

_____

_____

_____

Did your definition include physical well-being? That is a common response. But it is important to realize that wellness is often more complex, as it includes several essential dimensions. If wellness relates to our bodies, then thoughts and feelings are worthwhile to consider, since what affects our health goes beyond the body. Do you feel your best when you set aside time for your loved ones? Do you feel healthy when you are mindful of your nutrition? Or perhaps you feel happiest when you dedicate a portion of your energy to a higher power.

YOUR WELLNESS DOMAINS

Are any of these common areas of wellness important for your well-being? Circle the ones that resonate with you.

Career	Friendship	Mental
Community	Gender	Nature
Creative	Intellectual	Nutrition
Cultural	Interpersonal and Intrapersonal Relationships	Physical
Educational	Leisure	Sexual
Emotional	Life Planning	Social
Family	Love	Spiritual
Financial		Work

Write all of your wellness domains here. Including the domains circled on the previous page may be helpful. However, it is your wellness. Add in your own wellness categories. Choose words that resonate with you.

Using the words you brainstormed above, divide your wellness into five to eight categories. Having a clear understanding of your wellness domains will help you to foster your well-being.

MY CURRENT WELLNESS

Now, think about your wellness in a given week. Ideally your wellness would align with the time and energy you spend on each domain per week. However, if you are disconnected from your wellness, it's possible that most of your time is taken up with other activities that do not correlate with your wellness categories.

Create a snapshot of your current wellness. Using your wellness categories, create a pie chart to show how you spend a typical week. Then, use the snapshot to answer the questions that follow.

Are some parts of your time going to something beyond your wellness?

_____

_____

If so, is that acceptable for you?

_____

_____

Are you happy with the division of your energy?

_____

_____

What areas would you like to increase?

_____

_____

How will you do that?

_____

_____

Are there areas you would like to decrease?

_____

_____

MY FUTURE WELLNESS

"You can't cross the sea merely by standing and staring at the water."
—Rabindranath Tagore

Considering your reflection from My Current Wellness (page 55), what would you like your wellness wheel to look like?

What are your impressions of your future wellness?

_____

_____

Did your categories remain the same or did you need to remove unwarranted domains and/or add new domains?

_____

_____

Do you believe your ideal wellness is feasible? Why, or why not?

_____

_____

Are there some challenges to achieving this?

_____

_____

STRIVING FOR BALANCE

In order to shift from your current snapshot to your ideal wellness wheel, what do you need to decrease and what do you need to increase? For example, you may notice that you need to make more space for time to yourself. Relatedly, you may observe that the social piece of your wellness is bigger than it needs to be for balance. Hence, you may try to adjust time from your social domain to fuel your personal wellness.

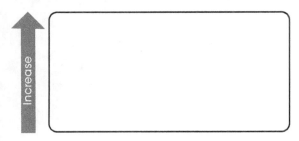
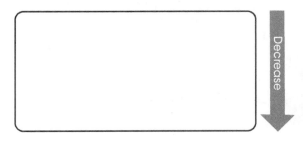

Now that you know what your ideal wellness ratio looks like and what may need to change to get there, think about all of the possible things you can do to fill each wellness slice. You don't need to master meditation hour or escape to an island paradise to fill your wellness wheel. Of course, those can be considered; however, brainstorm tangible tasks that you can easily do in your everyday life. Bigger items are encouraged, but remember that small efforts can add up as well.

Divide the space below into each domain and consider all of your options.

MY WELLNESS PLAN

Now that you have a variety of ways to fuel your wellness domains, it will be helpful to think about how to incorporate these aspects of wellness into your everyday life.

In loving myself, these are the things I would like to do for my wellness.

Daily:

_____

_____

_____

_____

Twice a week:

_____

_____

_____

_____

Weekly:

_____

_____

_____

_____

Every other week:

_____

_____

_____

_____

Monthly:

_____

_____

_____

_____

At least once per season:

_____

_____

_____

_____

At least once a year:

_____

_____

_____

_____

SELF-LOVE DATE

"To love oneself is the beginning of a life-long romance."
—Oscar Wilde

Tending to your wellness provides the foundation for self-care and shows that you recognize your self-worth. To maintain your self-esteem and foster your happiness, it is important to treat yourself similarly to how you treat the special people in your life. Just as you wouldn't think twice about spending the time, energy, and effort to show appreciation for a loved one, you can do the same for yourself.

Consider your wellness and how you receive love. Take a moment to plan a date just for you. Think about what you might need, where it may take place, and when it could occur.

_____

_____

_____

_____

_____

_____

_____

_____

_____

_____

_____

100 WAYS TO COPE

Wellness and coping are similar, yet different. Wellness is comprised of your general efforts to maintain a positive well-being. Coping is comprised of the active methods you use when faced with stressors. Ideally, wellness would occur whether or not you're having a difficult day. Coping skills can be similar to those you use for general wellness, but often they are intentional and specific ways to handle the effects of a hardship. For example, spending time with your friends may be an important part of your social wellness. However, if you are faced with a difficult decision, you may choose to cope by calling a friend to have him/her help broaden your perspectives, calm your fears, and encourage you to make the right choice.

Here are 100 examples of things you can do to cope:

❏ 1. Attend a concert

❏ 2. Attend a sporting event

❏ 3. Bake

❏ 4. Breathe deeply

❏ 5. Call a helpline

❏ 6. Call an old friend

❏ 7. Clean

❏ 8. Color

❏ 9. Cook

❏ 10. Craft

❏ 11. Create an affirmation

❏ 12. Create boundaries

❏ 13. Dance

❏ 14. De-clutter

❏ 15. Donate

❏ 16. Do something nice for someone else

❏ 17. Draw

❏ 18. Eat a healthy meal

❏ 19. Exercise

❏ 20. Embrace silence

❏ 21. Forgive someone

❏ 22. Garden

❏ 23. Get a massage

❏ 24. Get a manicure

❏ 25. Get a pedicure

❏ 26. Give a compliment

❏ 27. Give a hug

❏ 28. Go outside

❏ 29. Groom yourself

❏ 30. Hydrate

❏ 31. Journal

❏ 32. Knit

❏ 33. Light a candle

❏ 34. Light incense

❏ 35. Listen to music

❏ 36. Listen to a podcast

❏ 37. Listen to your favorite song

❏ 38. Look at old photos

❏ 39. Look at the sky

❏ 40. Make a gratitude list

❏ 41. Make a positive playlist

❏ 42. Make a mandala

❏ 43. Make travel plans

❏ 44. Meditate

❏ 45. Meet a friend

❏ 46. Nap

❏ 47. Organize

❏ 48. Paint

❏ 49. Plan a trip

❏ 50. Play a game

❏ 51. Play a sport

❏ 52. Play an instrument

❏ 53. Play videogames

❏ 54. Play with a pet

- [ ] 55. Practice assertiveness
- [ ] 56. Practice mindfulness
- [ ] 57. Practice safe sex
- [ ] 58. Pray
- [ ] 59. Read
- [ ] 60. Read affirmations
- [ ] 61. Relaxation techniques
- [ ] 62. Rearrange furniture
- [ ] 63. Rest
- [ ] 64. Run
- [ ] 65. Say no to negativity
- [ ] 66. Set a goal
- [ ] 67. Sew
- [ ] 68. Sing
- [ ] 69. Smile
- [ ] 70. Solve a puzzle

- [ ] 71. Spend time in nature
- [ ] 72. Spend time with positive people
- [ ] 73. Stretch
- [ ] 74. Study
- [ ] 75. Take a bath
- [ ] 76. Take a break
- [ ] 77. Take a mental health day
- [ ] 78. Take pictures
- [ ] 79. Take a shower
- [ ] 80. Take your vitamins
- [ ] 81. Therapy
- [ ] 82. Think positively
- [ ] 83. Try a DIY project
- [ ] 84. Try a new recipe
- [ ] 85. Unplug from social media

- [ ] 86. Use a fidget toy
- [ ] 87. Use essential oils
- [ ] 88. Use visualization
- [ ] 89. Volunteer
- [ ] 90. Walk
- [ ] 91. Watch funny videos
- [ ] 92. Watch the sunset
- [ ] 93. Watch your favorite movie
- [ ] 94. Watch your favorite show
- [ ] 95. Work
- [ ] 96. Write a letter
- [ ] 97. Write a poem
- [ ] 98. Write a song
- [ ] 99. Write a story
- [ ] 100. Yoga

COPING SKILLS

Are there additional coping skills you would like to add?

_____

_____

_____

_____

1. In the 100 examples of coping strategies, check each box that you have used to cope in the past.

2. Use a strikethrough to show which coping skills are unhelpful for you.

3. Place a star next to each coping skill that has been helpful for you.

4. As you try these skills, update the list over time.

JOURNALING

Journaling is a reflective strategy. Various styles of journaling can allow you to nonjudgmentally explore your thoughts, feelings, and behaviors, confront deep conflicts, and experience a curative self-loving escape. So far you have had a few chances to use journaling methods. In Chapter 2, Self-Awareness, you had the opportunity to utilize an open-ended journal prompt. Also, at the end of each chapter you have had the opportunity to use journaling to review and reflect on the topics in each section. In a smaller form, many of the activities call for a small, succinct reflection. As you can see, journaling methods can range from general to specific, with several examples provided below.

Open-ended: This type of journaling is intentionally broad to allow for enhanced exploration. For example, you may choose to reflect on self-love without constraining your exploration to a specific prompt.

Release: Also known as a stream-of-consciousness prompt, this is an open-ended type of journaling in which you intentionally purge every thought that comes to mind in that moment. Yes, even the thought "I don't have any more thoughts" gets released if it comes to mind. This style is often effective with a timer set for a short amount of time. If you've had a heated argument with someone but need to go back to work, you may use this method to release and help you to reset.

Review: Similar to the prompts at the end of each chapter in this book, a review journal can help you review a particular event, theme, or topic. While doing so, you are able to revisit the topic and take your reflection deeper. This type of journal is commonly used at the end of the day. For example, you may wish to reflect daily on your self-care practices.

Plan: A planning journal allows you to brainstorm your aspirations. You can explore possible methods to help you tangibly achieve your hopes and dreams. This method works well in conjunction with the review style of journaling, as you can reflect on what has occurred and how to improve over time.

Gratitude: A gratitude journal generally consists of open-ended prompts that are broadly focused on what you are thankful for. However, you may choose to explore specific realms of gratitude. For example, for one entry you could reflect on things you are grateful to have achieved and in another you could focus on the people you are grateful to have in your life.

What type of journaling do you enjoy?

_____

_____

_____

_____

CREATIVE SELF-CARE

"Creativity is intelligence having fun."
—Albert Einstein

Although everyone can benefit from self-care, not everyone benefits from the same types of self-care activities. The 100 Ways to Cope on page 62 are common ways that people practice tending to their needs; however, it can be helpful to tailor your self-care tasks to your individual identity. For example, someone who loves understanding how things work could find tinkering with a gadget peaceful and enjoyable. Someone who loves seeking adventure could find it fulfilling for their needs to check off skydiving from his or her bucket list. These examples are personalized, and although others could share in their enjoyment, they're not necessarily common coping mechanisms, but still just as helpful.

Reflect on who you are. See page 42, My Mission Statement, for some perspective.

What are the creative ways that you may cope?

_____

_____

_____

_____

_____

_____

_____

_____

LISTENING TO YOUR EMOTIONS

Feelings can serve as practical, powerful signals to help you recognize when you are in need of self-care. The ability to recognize this signal can help you in your self-love journey. You may find that certain coping skills may work better for some emotions over others. (See page 18, Emotional Awareness.)

Place a corresponding coping skill in each box below. Example: If you know that calling a loved one helps to lift your spirits, then you may wish to put "call a loved one" in the "sad" section.

Even when you are unclear about your current feelings, tuning into the emotions you wish to have can help you select the appropriate coping skill.

Sad	Stupid	Jealous	Ashamed
Inferior	Sleepy	Annoyed	Anxious
Bored	Hurt	Discouraged	Disgusted

Place a corresponding coping skill in each box below.

Example: If you know that taking a warm water bath helps to calm you, then you may wish to put "take a bath" in the "relaxed" section.

Relaxed	Thankful	Confident	Valuable
Satisfied	Creative	Playful	Daring
Aware	Respected	Amused	Proud

COPING TOOLKIT

Challenges are a normal part of life. One self-loving practice is to proactively prepare your coping kit, or go-to coping skills that are effective for you. Further, you have the opportunity to decipher the right skill for the right context. You wouldn't use a hammer when you need a screwdriver, and coping skills may also have specific purposes. Taking the time to equip yourself with effective coping skills helps you to be well-aware, prepared, and more likely to cope effectively.

What was the last difficult situation you encountered?

_____

_____

_____

How did you cope?

_____

_____

_____

What tools are presently in your kit?

_____

_____

_____

What tools have you tried that are not for you, and may not belong in your kit?

_____

_____

_____

What tools would you like to add to your kit?

_____

_____

_____

BAD-DAY BAND-AID

"Our greatest glory is not in never falling, but in rising every time we fall."
—Confucius

A bad-day Band-Aid is a helpful item to place in your coping kit. Proactively considering your coping skills can help you manage, achieve balance, and move a step closer to happiness. It's helpful to have a wide list of coping skills to tailor to any given situation. All coping skills are not created equal, and they can vary from person to person.

It is helpful to know what coping skills are effective for you. While it is helpful to have a selection, your bad-day Band-Aid is your go-to coping method for a difficult day.

What is your bad-day Band-Aid?

_____

_____

_____

_____

MY COMFORT ZONE

Your environment can play an important role in your self-care. It is helpful to consider what type of setting works well for your wellness. In your safe space you feel comfortable and relaxed. In your comfort zone you are able to let your guard down and be vulnerable. You may already have a place in mind, or you may have to create a comfort zone.

In the space below, sketch your safe space. Be sure to include key items or attributes.

EXPLORING MY SUPPORT SYSTEM

Positive people provide a wealth of support for self-care and wellness, particularly when you are depleted. Your social support system is made up of the people you can turn to for help. Individuals who care for you may signal your self-care necessities when they see something in your blind spot. Furthermore, they can care for, encourage, assist, guide, and motivate you along your self-love journey.

Begin to explore the realms of your social support in the space below. List all of the people that have or can help to support your wellness, self-care, and self-love.

CHALLENGING SELF-CARE

"Do the difficult things while they are easy and do the great things while they are small. A journey of a thousand miles must begin with a single step."

—Lao Tzu

Not all parts of self-care are pleasant, but at the end of the day, they are all positive. A critical component in self-care is the self-awareness to recognize that there may be gaps in your wellness. Furthermore, self-care requires the courage of self-exploration to improve your self-knowledge. Hence, self-care can include challenging tasks that are for the betterment of your overall self.

Examples of challenging self-care:

- Setting boundaries with others

- Creating limits for yourself

- Confronting someone who consistently hurts you

What are the challenging tasks in your self-care?

_____

_____

_____

_____

What do you need to empower you to tackle these difficult duties?

_____

_____

_____

_____

* * *

Self-care is an essential self-love practice. In this chapter you were able to delve into methods of maintaining your well-being, from highlighting practical coping skills to recognizing deeper needs that require fulfillment. Self-care is foundational in loving yourself, and maintaining your self-care is an ongoing way to love yourself.

CHAPTER 5

SELF-ESTEEM

It is common to confuse self-esteem with terms such as confidence, efficacy, and worth. Although these terms are related, it is important to recognize what self-esteem is by itself. Your self-esteem is how you appraise your worth, and how you think, feel, and act because of your assessment. Low self-esteem is associated with a poor valuation whereas high self-esteem signifies a strong sense of worthiness. Hence, your esteem consists of beliefs you hold about yourself. In essence, it is how you judge your personal value.

Low self-esteem is associated with stress, depression, prejudice, materialism, relationship insecurity, and poor coping. Low self-esteem is a known risk factor in the development of mental health problems such as eating disorders, anxiety, and depression.

While having healthy self-esteem is deemed essential, some common misunderstandings arise around it. For one, high self-esteem is often interpreted as the gold standard. In reality, a secure sense of esteem fluctuates. While individuals with very low self-esteem are often more vulnerable, on the opposite end of the spectrum, an individual with very high self-esteem could be defensive and irrational. Additionally, the need for healthy self-esteem is often acknowledged in earlier years, adolescence in particular. But tending to self-esteem is crucial throughout the lifespan.

It is important to see self-esteem for what it truly is and to avoid confusing it with similar concepts or diluting it with false associations. Building a healthy sense of self-esteem is a helpful practice of self-love. Fostering your self-esteem helps you to better understand yourself and develop a healthier sense of identity. Furthermore, seeing self-esteem as an assessment of our worth helps us to consider humanity and universal rights. In honoring your worth in your purest form, you respect the value of others as well. Hence, self-esteem can be a helpful factor in your personal journey of self-love, yet the benefits may have a broader impact on the world around you.

ACKNOWLEDGING MY WORTH

*"The world needs a sense of worth, and it will achieve it
only by its people feeling that they are worthwhile."*
—Fred Rogers

Take a moment and consider your worth. As discussed in What Self-Love Isn't (page 9), acknowledging your self-worth does not make you prideful, selfish, or entitled. Strip away your titles, achievements, and experiences. You, as a human being, are worthy. By just being alive you are valid, important, and enough.

I am worthy of...

1. _____

2. _____

3. _____

4. _____

5. _____

6. _____

7. _____

8. _____

9. _____

10. _____

11. _____

12. _____

13. _____

14. _____

15. _____

16. _____

17. _____

18. _____

19. _____

20. _____

ME FOR THREE

Self-esteem encompasses beliefs we hold about ourselves. This can include adjectives that describe personality, appearance, habits, interests, roles, and experiences.

Set a timer for three minutes. In that time, write as many attributes about yourself as you can in the space below.

MY PERSONAL QUALITIES

There are typically three ways in which we think about ourselves: positive, negative, or neutral. You may not realize when your mental tone turns from positive to negative. Sometimes thinking negatively can become a habit. However, the way you see yourself affects you. Think about your self-evaluations like a bank account. When you think negatively about yourself, you withdraw from your account, whereas positive thoughts can enhance your balance. Recognizing these internal transactions is helpful to heighten your awareness and empower you to monitor your self-love.

Place your brainstormed attributes from Me for Three in the chart on the next page in accordance with how you view these characteristics. For example you may place optimistic in positive, talkative in neutral, and bossy in negative. Keep in mind that your categories should be based on your own perspectives. For example, while others may see being talkative as a skill, others may see it as negative; what matters the most is that you may view it as both.

POSITIVE	NEUTRAL	NEGATIVE

While reflecting, it is possible that you may have recognized qualities you did not remember in the three-minute range. Feel free to add more to have a thorough view of you.

SUBJECTIVE SUPERLATIVES

One way to learn about your personal qualities is to receive feedback from others. Feedback (see page 32) is a helpful tool to broaden your perspective. However, sometimes you can become too dependent on what others think and you may lose sight of your own views.

In the space below, take a moment to give yourself credit for your awesome traits. These can range from simply highlighting a strength to warmly rewarding yourself with a superlative. You can use the prompts below and make your own.

When you consider things that other people have said about you that may be true, feel free to add to the personal qualities chart.

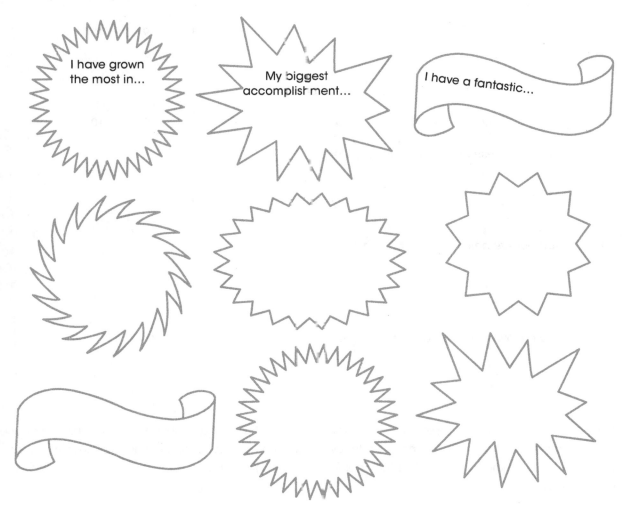

CONFIDENT PEOPLE

Confidence can be defined as the trust you have in yourself. Can you think of three people that you believe have a large amount of self-trust?

On a scale of 1 to 10, with one being little to no confidence and 10 being as confident as possible, draw a symbol on the number that corresponds with each person you select.

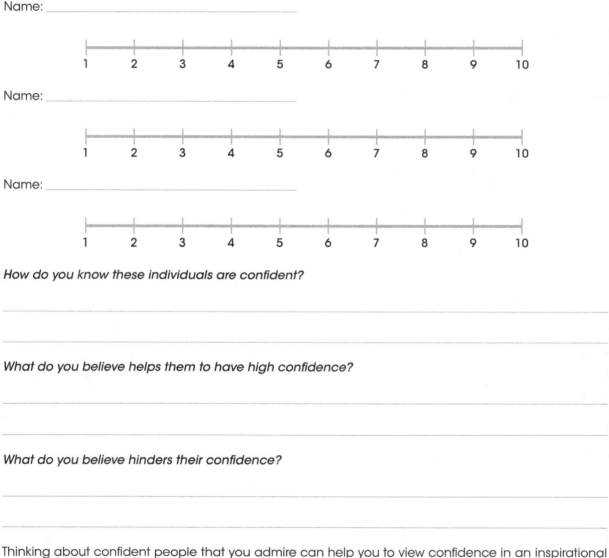

Name: _____

```
  1    2    3    4    5    6    7    8    9    10
```

Name: _____

```
  1    2    3    4    5    6    7    8    9    10
```

Name: _____

```
  1    2    3    4    5    6    7    8    9    10
```

How do you know these individuals are confident?

_____

_____

What do you believe helps them to have high confidence?

_____

_____

What do you believe hinders their confidence?

_____

_____

Thinking about confident people that you admire can help you to view confidence in an inspirational and non-threatening way. Observing confidence in people you know can help you to set examples for yourself. Also, examining what fosters their confidence can allow you to consider methods to improve your own self-trust.

MY SELF-CONFIDENCE

"Go confidently in the direction of your dreams. Live the life you have imagined."

—Henry David Thoreau

Think about a time in your past in which you did not trust yourself. Describe that event below.	Think about a time in your past in which you trusted yourself. Describe that event below.
Looking back, did you have any reasons to trust yourself?	Looking back, what reasons did you have to trust yourself?
Did anything stand in your way at the time?	Did anything cause your trust to waver?

If you compare and contrast these events, what do you notice?

_____

_____

_____

How confident are you in this present moment? Draw a symbol on your selected number on the scale of 1 to 10 below, with 1 being little to no confidence and 10 being as confident as possible.

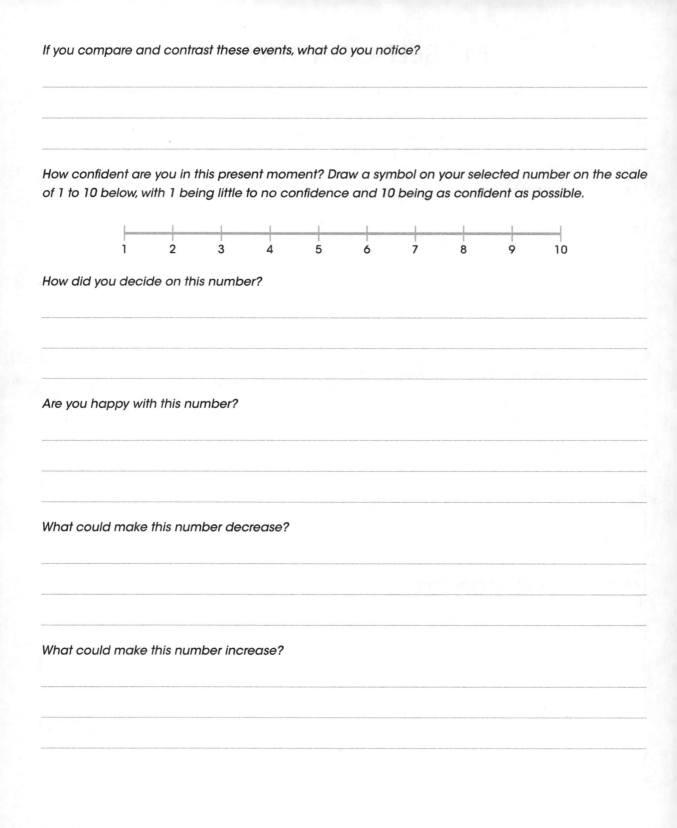

1   2   3   4   5   6   7   8   9   10

How did you decide on this number?

_____

_____

_____

Are you happy with this number?

_____

_____

_____

What could make this number decrease?

_____

_____

_____

What could make this number increase?

_____

_____

_____

UNDERSTANDING SELF-EFFICACY

"It always seems impossible until it's done."

—Nelson Mandela

When thinking about your current confidence level, you may have found it difficult to pick a number from 1 to 10. This prompt encouraged self-awareness. Since self-esteem is a personal assessment, you may have struggled to rid yourself of outside influences and connect to your inner voice. Even when you were empowered to make your own analysis, you may have found yourself recognizing how broad confidence can be.

Another way to look at your self-trust is to consider your belief in your abilities, otherwise known as self-efficacy. No one is perfect, and regardless of your hard work, intentions, and effort, you can't do it all. You have both strengths and weaknesses. Using the concept of self-efficacy allows you to better understand your skillsets, deficits, and all that lies in between.

Self-efficacy allows you to honor your talents. In the areas in which you may be lacking, acknowledging the lens of efficacy over confidence allows for a flexible way of seeing yourself. For example, you might have low self-efficacy about your ability to run a marathon tomorrow and to complete it within 4 hours and 20 minutes. This does not mean that running a marathon in 4 hours and 20 minutes is impossible, it just means that if you were not previously training for such an endeavor, it would be a bit absurd to set such a standard. Your confidence may be low, but recognizing that it is understandable that you do not have certain abilities needed to take on this feat tomorrow is a healthier perspective. On the other hand, if you have been training for a marathon for months, previously completed a marathon in a similar time frame, and just so happen to have a race day tomorrow, perhaps you have high self-efficacy in this area.

MY SELF-EFFICACY

For each of the following prompts, consider the range of your self-efficacy from low to high. For each ability, place a symbol along the line to indicate your level. Provide a rationale for your ability judgment.

Drive a car

LOW .... HIGH

Take a six-hour flight

LOW ·· HIGH

_____

Teach a math class

LOW ·· HIGH

_____

Host a party

LOW ·· HIGH

_____

Create a budget

LOW ·· HIGH

_____

Change a diaper

LOW ·· HIGH

_____

Do a cartwheel

LOW ·· HIGH

_____

Alter a pair of pants

LOW ·· HIGH

_____

_____

Build a bird house

LOW ·· HIGH

_____

_____

ROLE MODELS

Role models can be a resource to improve your self-esteem. Earlier you considered individuals that you believe are confident (see page 78, Confident People). As you delve further, you may be able to use their self-trust as an example of how to foster your own.

Individuals who are familiar to you can be helpful role models as you may have the ability to inquire about their own self-love journey. For example, a fiend that you may believe has high self-esteem may be willing to discuss their path toward healthy self-esteem. From that conversation, you may be able to find insightful points to consider for your own process. A role model does not need to be limited to someone you know personally. Historical figures, fictional characters, and influential celebrities could have the potential to inspire you and assist you in boosting your self-esteem as well.

Use the lines below to list the names of the people you admire.

_____

_____

_____

_____

_____

_____

What self-esteem lessons can you learn from the individuals you listed?

_____

_____

_____

_____

_____

MY INNER DIALOGUE

"All our dreams can come true, if we have the courage to pursue them."
—Walt Disney

In order to truly consider your esteem, confidence, and efficacy, you must be able to tune into your inner dialogue, or self-talk. Listening to your internal chatter can help you to notice your personal assessments. The messages included in your internal script may range from positive to negative. While intently attending to your self-talk, you may also notice that the content could be affecting your esteem, confidence, and efficacy. Like heavy weights, your negative self-talk could be dragging down your assessment of yourself. On the other hand, positive, helpful thoughts can help you to feel empowered and unrestrained. Being mindful of your self-talk is a practice of self-love.

Some examples of negative self-talk:

I'll never be able to find time for myself.

I can't do anything right.

No one likes to be around me.

Considering the examples above, what are some negative statements you have said to yourself?

_____

_____

_____

_____

Oftentimes our inner chatter can go unnoticed. However, negative self-talk hinders our self-love. Paying attention to our thoughts can help us to recognize when unacceptable negative thoughts are hijacking our cognitions and creating barriers to self-love. Also, from recognizing our negative statements, we can be empowered to transform these patterns into positive thoughts and foster self-love in the process.

UNHELPFUL THINKING

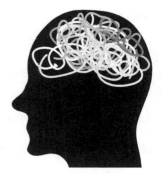

Negative self-talk can often be distorted or irrational. Nevertheless, regardless of accuracy, negative self-talk can be a powerful and deleterious force on self-esteem. Therefore, addressing and transforming negative inner dialogue can be a self-loving practice.

The first step in addressing negative self-talk is to become aware that the given thought is unhelpful. This may seem simple; however, lack of intentionality means lack of regulation for unhelpful self-talk. Without realizing the problem and its influence, you can unknowingly surrender your self-esteem to the strong influence of negative self-talk. After understanding the influence of negative inner dialogue and catching such unhelpful statements, you may have the opportunity to widen your perspective and alter your thinking.

Some common styles of distorted thinking can be seen in negative self-talk. Understanding these irrational thinking patterns can help you to illuminate an unhelpful internal statement and motivate you to change the statement. The process of changing a statement from negative to positive can improve self-esteem and overall self-love.

Consider these examples of distorted thinking. Check off each example that you have used.

❑ Filtering: seeing things through a limited lens while ignoring a broader perspective.

   For example: *Good things never happen to me.*

❑ Overgeneralization: widely applying a single view and expecting it to be true for all situations.

   For example: *Of course she doesn't want to talk to me, no one ever does.*

❑ Labeling: arriving at a particular judgment based on skewed and limited information. This can include name-calling or reducing someone or something to a singular title or perspective.

   For example: *I didn't do well on that exam, I'm stupid.*

❑ Jumping to conclusions: prematurely arriving at an answer without having sufficient evidence.

   For example: *He hasn't responded yet, he must be angry with me.*

- Catastrophizing: assuming the worst-case scenario is likely while ignoring other possibilities.

  For example: *I'll never get married.*

- Polarized thinking: seeing things dichotomously, or as one way or the other, without acknowledging the gray area that often lies between.

  For example: *I didn't get the promotion; I'm a failure.*

- Personalization: taking things personally or assuming responsibility for things that are beyond your control.

  For example: *She didn't say hello to me, she must not like me.*

- Should/ought/must: Enforcing unrealistic, high expectations on yourself or others that make it difficult to attain.

  For example: *I should have been a better partner, then I wouldn't be single.*

- Magnification: exaggerating the influence of a detail or situation.

  For example: *That was the worst presentation, but the audience enjoyed it.*

- Minimization: reducing or ignoring the emphasis of a detail or situation.

  For example: *Thank you for complimenting me on my award; it isn't that big of a deal though.*

- Mind-reading: assuming to know what others think or feel without considering the facts.

  For example: *She thinks I'm an idiot.*

- Fortunetelling: having a strong conviction that something will happen. Predicting the future without sufficient evidence.

  For example: *I'm not going to get the job.*

- Emotional reasoning: being misled by your feelings. Allowing your emotions to convince you of what is occurring in reality.

  For example: *I feel scared, I must be in danger.*

FORMULAS FOR COUNTERING

"If you don't like something, change it. If you can't change it, change your attitude."

—Maya Angelou

Recognizing that a thought is distorted may prompt you to change your thinking process. How can you transform the examples of unhelpful thinking listed previously into helpful thoughts? Using your self-knowledge (see page 24), create formulas for each thinking error to help you modify your thinking process and improve your self-talk.

Filtering	
Overgeneralization	
Labeling	
Jumping to conclusions	
Catastrophizing	
Polarized thinking	
Personalization	
Should/ought/must	
Magnification	
Minimization	
Mind-reading	
Fortunetelling	
Emotional reasoning	

Reflect on the examples of distorted thinking that you checked off on pages 85–86. For each, provide a sample statement that has crossed your mind at one point in time. If possible, try to use a statement that has affected you recently and/or has influenced you greatly. Then, use the formulas you created on the previous page to help you arrive at a kinder thought.

Example: _____

Type of Unhealthy Thinking: _____

Self-Loving Thought: _____

Example: _____

Type of Unhealthy Thinking: _____

Self-Loving Thought: _____

Example: _____

Type of Unhealthy Thinking: _____

Self-Loving Thought: _____

Example: _____

Type of Unhealthy Thinking: _____

Self-Loving Thought: _____

Example: _____

Type of Unhealthy Thinking: _____

Self-Loving Thought: _____

Example: _____

Type of Unhealthy Thinking: _____

Self-Loving Thought: _____

Example: _____

Type of Unhealthy Thinking: _____

Self-Loving Thought: _____

CHALLENGING UNHELPFUL THINKING

"With the new day comes new strength and new thoughts."
—Eleanor Roosevelt

Self-awareness is key in recognizing when you may be experiencing distorted thoughts (see Self-Awareness on page 16). Without this recognition, you may struggle to realize when there is a pertinent need to change your flawed thinking. Furthermore, not all forms of negative self-talk qualify as unhelpful thinking. You may have negative thoughts cross your mind that you know are negative but they may seem logical and helpful (see page 85).

In the lines below, provide an example of a negative thought that has deeply affected you. If possible, try to choose a thought that still affects you today. It may be helpful for you to select a thought that you may struggle to change, even after applying the formulas you tailored.

Considering the negative statement you provided, answer the following questions. They can help you to challenge your unhelpful thinking.

	YES	NO
Is this a self-loving statement?	☐	☐
Is this thought helpful?	☐	☐
Is it in my control?	☐	☐
Is there someone I can seek feedback from on the accuracy of this thought?	☐	☐
Am I blaming myself unnecessarily?	☐	☐
Am I holding myself to unrealistic standards?	☐	☐
Am I jumping to conclusions?	☐	☐
Am I taking this personally when it may not be a personal matter?	☐	☐
Am I making assumptions?	☐	☐
Are there exceptions to this negative statement?	☐	☐
Is this thought accurate?	☐	☐
Do I have evidence to support this thought?	☐	☐
Can I test my assumptions?	☐	☐
Could there be other perspectives?	☐	☐
Are there other ways to think about it?	☐	☐
Would I say this to a friend?	☐	☐

PETAL PERSPECTIVES: IMPROVING POSITIVE SELF-TALK

The flowers below can be used to help you begin to reconsider and challenge your unhelpful thoughts. Reflect on your inner dialogue and consider your commonly used negative statements. For each flower, place one example of negative self-talk in the center. Then, use the petals to brainstorm ways to counter that negative thought. You may find it helpful to consider the formulas you created as well as the questions to challenge negative self-talk. Try your best to create positive and powerful perspectives that are infused with self-love!

ME MESSAGES

Sometimes self-talk may not necessarily be distorted or negative, but can still be unhelpful. This may happen when the statement isn't congruent with who you are. (See page 46, Inner Conflict.)

Since these messages float around in our heads we assume they are our messages. However, these may be messages that we adapted from other people. It is possible that these statements can be practical points of feedback, but it is also possible that they are unhelpful messages that conflict with our true self and cause distressing inner dialogue (See page 29, Finding Blind Spots.)

Take a moment to think about your self-talk. What are some examples of statements that are truly your own and what are examples of statements that may be influenced by others?

ME	OTHERS

TRASH TOSS

You can't control others' statements, but you can consider when a message is consistent with who you are, helpful, and self-loving. Some of the statements in the "other" section above can be feedback that can be used to prompt self-exploration (see Chapter 3) and self-growth (see Chapter 8). Highlighting some of the statements in this exercise may cause you to realize that they are not consistent with who you are. You may have unknowingly held on to useless negative statements that have inhibited your self-esteem. For example, you may be affected by inaccurate comments from a pushy past partner. Or, you may be pressured by unrealistic expectations you have received from societal standards.

When you realize a statement is both incongruent and unhelpful, it may be time to consider tossing these thoughts in the trash. What thoughts belong in the bin?

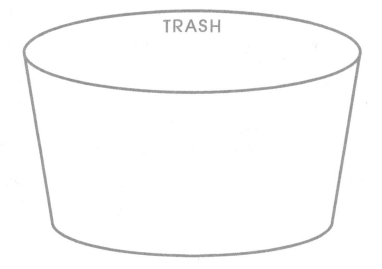

TRASH

BUILDING BLOCKS

You can increase your positive thoughts and improve your self-esteem by reflecting on your strengths, achievements, abilities, and successes. Taking the time to consider these truths can cause you to recognize your worth, improve your self-trust, and enhance your beliefs in yourself. The building blocks below can help you to build your self-esteem. The prompts can help you to lay the foundation of positive self-talk.

Feel free to use the blank boxes to expand on positive statements of your choice!

In the future I will...	People can count on me to...
I know I can trust myself to...	Even on my bad days I am still...

If I tried hard I could...

A pure strength of mine is...

Even though I didn't think I would succeed
at the time, I am happy that I...

I know that I can...

I like that I...

I am good at...

I have been able to...

I am capable of...

I am proud that I...

After a lot of hard work I...

MOTIVATIONAL MESSAGES

Motivational messages can help to fill a void in your self-esteem. Difficult days are inevitable; however, it is possible to find inspiration in those trying times, boost your self-esteem, and provide yourself the self-love you deserve. These useful words often arise from your loved ones, role models, or other people who've left an impression on you. Use the hearts below to write motivational messages that inspire you.

Here are examples of inspirational quotes. Select the ones that resonate with you, and hence could be useful for you.

- "With the new day comes new strength and new thoughts." —Eleanor Roosevelt

- "It always seems impossible until it's done." —Nelson Mandela

- "When you come to the end of your rope, tie a knot and hang on." —Franklin Roosevelt

- "We may encounter many defeats but we must not be defeated." —Maya Angelou

- "The pessimist sees difficulty in every opportunity. The optimist sees opportunity in every difficulty." —Winston Churchill

- "I hope you live a life you're proud of, and if you're not, I hope you have the courage to start over again." —F. Scott Fitzgerald

- "You can't go back and change the beginning, but you can start where you are and change the ending." —C. S. Lewis

Add your favorite inspirational quotes here:

_____

_____

_____

_____

_____

_____

_____

AFFIRMATIONS

Motivational messages can come from within you. Many times, these are the most powerful, as you are the expert in you. Affirmations are practical, positive self-talk statements that can empower you and boost your self-esteem.

Here are some examples. Select the ones that resonate with you:

I can learn from my mistakes.

Life is beautiful.

Practice over perfection.

Never give up.

I am powerful.

I can make a difference.

I am enough.

I am worthy of love.

I am lovable.

Positive mind, positive heart, positive life.

I believe in myself.

I choose kindness.

I can.

I am courageous.

I love myself.

Anything is possible.

I am fortunate.

I am ready.

Create an affirmation of your own:

_____

_____

_____

_____

Practice saying this to yourself at least one time per day.

POSITIVE PLAYLIST

"We are the music makers, and we are the dreamers of dreams."
—Arthur O'Shaughnessy

Music is powerful. It can lift you up at any time, but this is particularly impactful when you are down. When your self-esteem is low, listening to a good tune or two can help to boost your self-esteem. Therefore, turning up the volume when you are feeling depleted can be an act of self-love.

Create a positive playlist to help you turn up the dial when your self-esteem is low. Bonus points for singing, dancing, or playing along!

If you need help exploring the emotions that these songs evoke, you may find it helpful to revisit the 100 Feeling Words on page 17.

Song	
Artist	
This song makes me feel…	
This song is helpful because…	

Song	
Artist	
This song makes me feel…	
This song is helpful because…	

Song	
Artist	
This song makes me feel…	
This song is helpful because…	

Song	
Artist	
This song makes me feel…	
This song is helpful because…	

Song	
Artist	
This song makes me feel…	
This song is helpful because…	

Song	
Artist	
This song makes me feel…	
This song is helpful because…	

Song	
Artist	
This song makes me feel…	
This song is helpful because…	

* * *

How you view yourself can greatly affect your self-love. Negative thoughts can taint your view of your worth and can serve as obstacles in promoting self-loving practices. On the other hand, a positive mindset can help you to create a sturdy foundation to foster your self-loving practices.

CHAPTER 6

SELF-KINDNESS

Self-kindness is the skill of being friendly to yourself. Self-kindness is associated with happiness, optimism, curiosity, conscientiousness, intrinsic motivation, emotional intelligence, and well-being. Self-kindness can be helpful in reducing stress, anxiety, self-criticism, avoidance, and depression. It can include how you tend to your needs and practice self-care. It can also encompass your approach to a negative thought, feeling, prompt, or situation. For example, having the self-awareness to tune into your needs and practice self-care is a gesture of self-kindness. Your self-kindness is also demonstrated in times in which you are faced with hurdles in your path. During such times, treating yourself with care instead of judgment and criticism is a crucial act of self-love.

Self-kindness is the balance you strive for between being dedicated to personal growth yet mindful of the need to be accepting, compassionate, patient, and grateful along the way. A strong sense of self-kindness allows you to acknowledge difficulties as a normal part of life, and to respect yourself as you progress on your self-love journey.

You have already learned some helpful ways to practice self-kindness, such as challenging unhelpful thinking (page 89), creating motivational messages (page 94), or employing affirmations (page 95).

Thinking about the definition of self-kindness, how are you nice to you?

_____

_____

_____

_____

_____

_____

NICE NOTES

A simple way to show yourself kindness is by being affirming and encouraging (see Affirmations on page 95). Craft thoughtful messages and jot them on small notes. To see one of these kind reminders often, place it in an area in which you will see it repeatedly, or you may also choose to place it where you will see it infrequently, perhaps when you need your kindness the most.

Use the notes below to brainstorm your kind messages.

LOVE LETTER

"To say 'I love you' one must know first how to say the 'I.'"

—Ayn Rand

Self-love cannot happen without kindness. As you practice being kind to yourself, your love for yourself will surely grow as well. As your love grows for someone else, it becomes natural, and sometimes expected, to profess your feelings. Although you may recognize that self-love is important, you may not consider articulating your self-love.

Use the letter template below as an open-ended reflection to yourself. Free yourself from judgment and criticism and allow yourself to genuinely share the self-loving thoughts that come to mind.

Dear _____ ,

_____

_____

_____

_____

_____

_____

_____

_____

_____

_____

_____

Love, _____

ENCOURAGERS

It's important to be kind to yourself when you need it the most. In times when you find yourself struggling, you have the ability to encourage and be kind to yourself for the helpful, motivating momentum you need to propel yourself forward. Encouragement can vary from person to person. For some, a positive thought (see Affirmations, page 95) or vision board (see Vision Board, page 148) may be motivating, while for others, listening to their favorite song or a speech by their role model is beneficial.

What are some ways that you can encourage yourself?

THE BULLY VERSUS THE FRIEND

*"Friendship with oneself is all important, because without it
one cannot be friends with anyone else in the world."*
—Eleanor Roosevelt

Unchecked negative thoughts can link together to create a powerful inner voice. When this happens, your inner dialogue may be impulsive, aggressive, controlling, argumentative, and manipulative. Your internal tone shifts from being your encouraging friend to your very own bully.

Consider the characteristics of a bully. What are some things you may have said in the past to bully yourself? Before responding to this prompt, it may be helpful to consider your thoughts around the qualities you believe are negative (see My Personal Qualities, page 75).

_____

_____

_____

_____

If you heard someone saying such things to your friend, how would you respond?

_____

_____

_____

_____

If your loved ones heard someone saying such things to you, how would they respond?

_____

_____

_____

_____

In order to transform your inner tone from bullying to friendly, what promise do you need to make to yourself?

_____

_____

_____

_____

In order to maintain this promise, what feedback do you need to give yourself about your inner tone?

_____

_____

_____

_____

What do you need more of?

_____

_____

_____

_____

What do you need less of?

_____

_____

_____

_____

LETTING GO OF NEGATIVITY

Your self-talk is the inner dialogue that you have in your mind (see My Inner Dialogue on page 84). Previously, you learned the impact of negative thoughts and practiced transforming them to kinder statements. Sometimes the process of challenging an unhelpful thought is easier said than done. We tend to have blind spots (see page 29) and obstacles that make it more difficult to be kind to ourselves in some instances, even when we know that being nice to ourselves is the healthier, self-loving option.

The prompts below will help you consider how to begin to release negativity and improve your self-love.

Have you noticed any trends in your negative self-talk?

_____

_____

_____

_____

_____

What are the areas in which you would like to show yourself less criticism?

_____

_____

_____

_____

_____

ROOM FOR GROWTH

Highlighting your strengths is a self-loving practice that can improve your self-esteem. However, beyond recognizing the areas in which you excel, it is also important to recognize where there is room for growth. Typically we see these as negative qualities or weaknesses, but the truth is that these areas give us opportunities for personal development.

Circle the traits below that represent areas in which you have room for growth.

I'd like to be more...

Active	Gentle	Prudent	Straightforward
Adventurous	Helpful	Punctual	Thankful
Affectionate	Honest	Purposeful	Thorough
Alert	Hopeful	Quiet	Tidy
Amicable	Independent	Reflective	Tolerant
Attentive	Observant	Romantic	Trustworthy
Brave	Open-minded	Secure	Warm
Calm	Passionate	Sensitive	Wise
Charitable	Patient	Serious	Witty
Compassionate	Perceptive	Silly	
Cooperative	Personable	Sincere	
Empathetic	Practical	Spontaneous	

Take a moment to brainstorm where you have opportunities to improve and list them in the space below. You can use the qualities circled above and the traits on the list you previously created (page 76); or, you can add new opportunities for growth that can go beyond personality (e.g., I have room for growth in my time-management skills).

THE GRACIOUS GAP

Self-kindness is the practice of recognizing your capacity for growth, yet being gracious to yourself as you fill that gap. You do not need to inundate yourself in negativity as you acknowledge the void.

For example, I have room for growth in my leadership skills. However, I recently gained the courage at work to volunteer to be a team captain in our upcoming group task. I am also trying to be more assertive, as I recognize my words are valuable. Although I have room for growth in this area, a positive quality is that I want to make sure that everyone is heard and is cooperative.

FILLING IN THE GAP

Choose three of the opportunities you listed in the Room for Growth exercise on page 106 and practice graciously filling the gap.

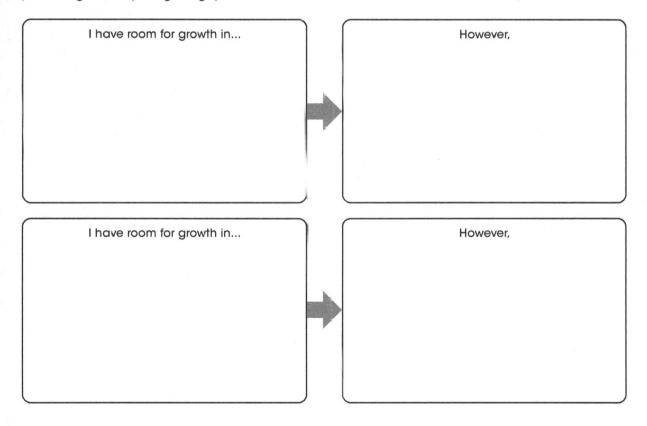

I have room for growth in...

However,

I have room for growth in...

However,

I have room for growth in...	However,

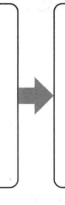

SETBACK SLINGSHOT

Setbacks are an inevitable part of life. Like a dance, we go through our journey trying our best to move forward; however, sidesteps and backtracking are to be expected. Yet during these moments we can become self-critical, judgmental, and mean to ourselves. If we could manage to be understanding, compassionate, and kind instead, we can empower ourselves to propel forward on our path once again.

Think of a time that you experienced a setback, and you criticized yourself. How could you have responded in a kinder way?

The prompts below may help you with this reflection.

I believe that…	Next time I can…
I learned that…	I didn't have control over…
This may have happened because…	From this experience…
I take full responsibility for…	In the future I hope to…
I tend to…	I wish I could have…

_____

_____

_____

_____

SELF-PATIENCE

"Every great dream begins with a dreamer. Always remember,
you have within you the strength, the patience, and the
passion to reach for the stars to change the world."
—Harriet Tubman

Impatience can serve as a hurdle in self-kindness. When you are eager to grow you may lack the tolerance for waiting. Rushing toward a finish line may cause you to lose sight of your purpose. Expectations can become stifling and, as you become frustrated, you begin to lose motivation. The power of patience allows you to be kind to yourself in your process. Reflect on your Mission Statement on page 42 as you contemplate ways to practice patience below.

In what areas do you need to practice patience?

_____

_____

_____

What helps your self-patience?

_____

_____

_____

What are the signs that you are becoming impatient?

_____

_____

_____

What can you do if you notice yourself becoming impatient?

_____

_____

_____

EMBRACING IMPERFECTION

"Have no fear of perfection—you'll never reach it."
—Salvador Dalí

A common trap that can bar your self-kindness is striving for perfection. Nothing and no one is perfect. Aiming for an impossible standard can trick you into believing that you are failing when, in reality, you could be making wonderful strides. To practice embracing imperfection, consider your wellness domains (page 53).

Select one of your wellness domains and write that label on the line below:

_____

To practice shunning perfectionism, you may simply choose to draw a line over, scribble over, or block out the word below:

PERFECT

Take a moment to visualize yourself achieving wellness in your selected area. What does a hopeful, yet realistic, standard of this aspect of your wellness look like? Use the space below to reflect. Feel free to explore this visualization with doodles or describe with words.

SELF-ACCEPTANCE

"The worst loneliness is to not be comfortable with yourself."

—Mark Twain

Practicing self-acceptance can be a helpful way to be kinder to yourself. Self-acceptance can help you fill the gracious gap, recover from setbacks, and release perfection. Beginning with an attuned self-awareness (see Chapter 2), your self-acceptance is a process in which you acknowledge and embrace both your strengths and weaknesses. It is a personal yet realistic point of view in which you find happiness in your strong suits, but you also achieve contentment with your limitations. Finding self-acceptance can help to shield you from self-judgment and release you from things you cannot control.

In the first box, describe a negative trait you may have. In the second box, write a counter that embodies self-acceptance.

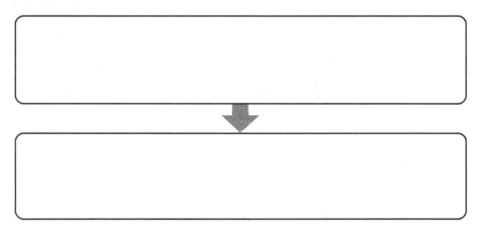

In the first box, describe an area in which you have room for growth (see Room for Growth traits you checked off on page 106). In the second box, write a counter that embodies self-acceptance.

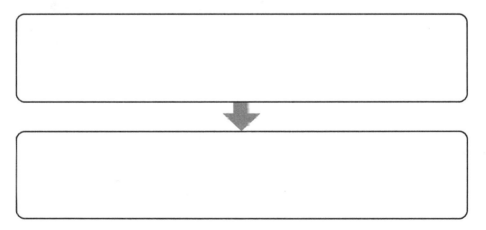

In the first box, describe a goal you have been striving towards for a long time. (See Vision Board on page 148.) You might want to jump back to this after reading Chapter 8: Self-Growth if you are having a hard time selecting a goal. In the second box, write a counter that embodies self-acceptance.

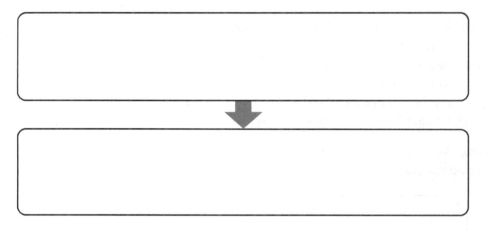

SELF-FORGIVENESS

"Forgiveness is a virtue of the brave."

—Indira Gandhi

Forgiveness is an essential step in permitting yourself to let go of a negative past occurrence. It is not to be confused with excusing, condoning, minimizing, or ignoring. Instead, as a self-loving act, self-forgiveness allows you to learn from your previous experiences, accept responsibility, take accountability, and set your intentions to learn and grow in the future. Self-forgiveness can be a difficult process, as both the forgiver and forgivee are within you. Another hurdle in self-forgiveness is reconciliation. Avoiding self-forgiveness comes with consequences. The inability to forgive yourself has been associated with anxiety, depression, and a weakened immune system. On the other hand, choosing to forgive yourself can decrease the negative effects of guilt, demonstrate your respect for yourself, and allow you to foster your growth.

PRACTICING SELF-FORGIVENESS

Think of a time you struggled to forgive yourself.

_____

_____

_____

What made it difficult to pardon yourself in this situation?

_____

_____

_____

What can you take accountability for in that situation?

_____

_____

_____

What was beyond your control in that situation?

_____

_____

_____

What lesson have you learned?

_____

_____

_____

What do you need to do in order to begin to let this go?

_____

_____

_____

How does this forgiveness relate to your self-love practice?

_____

_____

_____

Try this:

I forgive myself for [situation]. I know that I was [accountability statement]. In the future, [lesson learned]. I forgive myself because [self-love statement].

I forgive myself for

_____

_____

I know that I was

_____

_____

In the future,

_____

_____

I forgive myself because

_____

_____

GIFTS OF GRATITUDE

Practicing thankfulness can be a practical too in promoting self-kindness. Begin gratitude from within by highlighting something you appreciate about yourself. The kindness evoked from gratitude can emanate outward as well. For example, you may wish to acknowledge someone who has been caring to you or may be grateful for the community that you live in.

Each bit of gratitude is a gift. Draw a gift to represent all that you are grateful for. Begin with self-kindness by depicting presents you have given yourself. Then feel free to expand into gifts you have been given and wish to give as well.

* * *

Self-kindness is the compassionate practice of being a good friend to yourself. Just as you would stand up for a friend who is feeling sad, disrespected, or inadequate, you have the power to assure yourself as well. When you choose to be kinder to yourself, you diminish your tolerance for self-inflicted negativity. Your view on negativity and positivity may shift altogether. The kinder you are to yourself, the easier it is to allow positive statements to flow and nourish your soul. You are also able to create space to humbly deny perfection while you patiently practice acceptance, forgiveness, and gratitude.

SELF-KINDNESS REFLECTION

CHAPTER 7

SELF-RESPECT

Arising out of admiration, respect is demonstrated by acknowledging a person's dignity. As a basic human right, everyone deserves respect. Being equal to others, you are deserving of respect from others and from yourself as well. While respecting others is honorable, continually prioritizing respect of others over your own needs is not a self-loving act and can cause you to become mentally unwell. The respect you deserve is neither more or less than that of anyone else, but it is essential nevertheless.

Self-respect is an important virtue, as it includes your awareness of your worth, your ability to honor yourself, and your efforts to maintain your dignity. Self-respect is related to other essential important aspects of self-love, such as self-esteem and self-acceptance. It is important to note that self-respect is not to be confused with aggressiveness or entitlement.

A strong sense of self-respect helps you to better respect others and to be better respected by others. Having dignity in your identity allows you to set an example, particularly in terms of how you wish to be treated. It also allows you to protect yourself with gates that may open to permit you to connect with others and close to protect you from harm.

With self-respect, you recognize that you are priceless and cannot be objectified. You have a keen awareness of your personal values, which serve as an internal compass directing you on the path you wish to walk in your life journey. A connection to who you are provides the structure for you to build your identity. Nevertheless, honing your self-respect is a subjective experience that takes time to understand and implement. As you embark on this chapter of your journey, be sure to reflect on your unique identity and practice patience in the process.

Use the space below to brainstorm what you respect about yourself. You may find inspiration from past activities such as My Self-Efficacy (page 81), Nice Notes (page 100), and Subjective Superlatives (page 76).

VALUES

In order to respect yourself, you have to know not only what you believe in, but what you firmly represent. This can be achieved by exploring your values. Take a moment to reflect on who you are, and who you wish to be. Several of the values on the next page may apply to you, yet some may apply more strongly than others. Finding the values that adhere strongly to your sense of self can help you to define your core values and support your self-respect.

Earlier, you created a Mission Statement (see page 42) to help you define your purpose. It may be helpful to revisit that statement to help you reconnect with your values.

1. *Use each value to complete this sentence: "The value of _____ is very important to me." Reflect on the level to which you agree or disagree.*

2. *Use the key to place the appropriate symbols next to each value.*

VALUE KEY

– – –	– –	–	0	+	++	+++
Strongly Disagree	Disagree	Slightly Disagree	Neutral	Slightly Agree	Agree	Strongly Agree

You can use the empty lines to add in additional values that may apply to you.

_____ Achievement	_____ Humor	_____ Teamwork
_____ Altruism	_____ Learning	_____ Traditionalism
_____ Ambition	_____ Logic	_____ Versatility
_____ Awareness	_____ Love	_____ Wealth
_____ Balance	_____ Neutrality	_____
_____ Beauty	_____ Originality	_____
_____ Charity	_____ Peace	_____
_____ Cleanliness	_____ Politeness	_____
_____ Comfort	_____ Practicality	_____
_____ Communication	_____ Productivity	_____
_____ Connection	_____ Prosperity	_____
_____ Courage	_____ Quality	_____
_____ Dedication	_____ Recreation	_____
_____ Eccentricity	_____ Reflection	_____
_____ Fame	_____ Respect	_____
_____ Flexibility	_____ Restraint	_____
_____ Freedom	_____ Science	_____
_____ Fun	_____ Security	_____
_____ Generosity	_____ Selflessness	_____
_____ Happiness	_____ Sincerity	_____
_____ Health	_____ Solitude	_____
_____ Honesty	_____ Spirituality	_____
_____ Humility	_____ Stability	_____

CORE VALUES

As you refine your values, you are able to prioritize what matters the most to you. In the process, you are able to learn more about yourself. The better you know your true self, the more you are able to know your preferences, needs, limitations, and aspirations.

Take a moment to review the values that you marked with plus signs on the previous page. Place them in the corresponding boxes below. Rearrange the values as needed.

+	++	+++

While all of the values listed in the chart above are important to you, it is likely that those listed in the right column are your core values. From this section, choose your top five values that convey who you are as a person, what you believe in, and what you wish to embody in your lifetime.

The prompts below will to help you delve further into the connection that you have with each value.

Core value: _____

This is important to me because...

_____

_____

Without this value...

_____

_____

I uphold this value by...

_____

_____

Core value: _____

This is important to me because...

_____

_____

Without this value...

_____

_____

I uphold this value by...

_____

_____

Core value: _____

This is important to me because...

_____

_____

Without this value...

_____

_____

I uphold this value by...

_____

_____

Core value: _____

This is important to me because...

_____

_____

Without this value...

_____

_____

I uphold this value by...

_____

_____

Core value: _____

This is important to me because...

_____

_____

Without this value...

_____

_____

I uphold this value by...

_____

_____

PERSONAL COMMANDMENTS

"How you love yourself is how you teach others to love you."

—Rupi Kaur

Your core values give you an opportunity to honor your worth and serve as guidelines for your self-respect, allowing you to make informed rules to help you live you an empowered, self-loving life. These rules keep you aware of how you treat yourself, how to treat others, and how you wish to be treated.

To tailor your personal commandments in a way that honors your unique being, it may be helpful to consider your Core Values (page 120), Mission Statement (page 42), Affirmations (page 95), Motivational Messages (page 94), and Nice Notes (page 100) to gain inspiration.

Examples of personal commandments:

Be yourself.	Focus on the future.
Always be gracious.	I will do the best that I can.
Let things go.	Everyone is equal.

Create a personal commandment for each of your core values. Then, explain why you selected this phrase and what it means to you.

Personal Commandment 1:

_____

_____

Personal Commandment 2:

_____

_____

Personal Commandment 3:

_____

_____

Personal Commandment 4:

_____

_____

Personal Commandment 5:

_____

_____

CONGRUENCE

When there is consistency between what you believe in and how you behave, life tends to be easier and happier. On the other hand, when you live a life that is not in accordance with your values, it may cause you to experience an inner conflict (See Inner Conflict, page 46). When you are experiencing such internal friction, you are likely to develop negative feelings such as sadness, frustration, and resentment. For example, if one of your core values is honesty yet you cheated on an exam, your incongruence is likely to prompt negative sentiments such as guilt and regret.

Think of a time when your behavior aligned with your values. Explain how you achieved congruence and how it affected you.

_____

_____

_____

_____

Think of a time when your behavior did not align with your values. Explain what hindered your ability to achieve congruence and how it affected you.

_____

_____

_____

_____

Place one of your core values into each shape below. Reflect on your present status for each. Have you recently been behaving in a manner that is consistent with this core value? If so, draw an equivalent shape and explain how you are achieving congruence. If not, draw a disproportionate shape and explain what is holding you back from achieving congruence.

1.

2.

3.

4.

5.

If you have at least one value that is congruent with your behavior, explain how you plan to maintain that equivalence. On the other hand, if you have at least one value that is not aligned with your present lifestyle, explain what changes need to be made to assist realignment.

BOUNDARIES

"No one can make you feel inferior without your consent."
—Eleanor Roosevelt

Boundaries play an essential role in promoting and preserving self-respect. The mere decision to build boundaries is an act of self-love, as choosing to do so honors your worth and dignity. While this is a worthwhile task for people in general, the parameters to protect yourself tend to vary from person to person. As you reflect on your unique boundaries, it is important to devise strategies suited to uphold your needs.

Affirming your boundaries, particularly when they are tested, validates your sense of self-respect. In the process, it helps others acknowledge and respect you as well. The process does not conclude after the boundaries are created. Boundary management is an ongoing process in which you reevaluate your parameters and shift them as needed.

It can be difficult to balance the need for self-preservation with the temptation of self-sacrificing for the sake of others. From the first consideration that boundaries are needed to the times in which your limits are pushed, constructing boundaries can be a perplexing, yet purposeful, process.

Boundaries are often assumed to be demarcations set for social situations; however, self-respect begins with your treatment of yourself. Hence, in being responsible for your own behaviors, it is just as essential to formulate *intrapersonal boundaries* in addition to interpersonal boundaries. Your intrapersonal boundaries help you to regulate your reactions to your own prompts. The ability to be accountable for yourself by creating self-boundaries then helps to foster several self-loving domains such as self-awareness, self-acceptance, self-care, and self-growth.

What are some examples of boundaries that you have for yourself?

_____

_____

_____

What are some examples of self-boundaries you could benefit from creating?

_____

_____

_____

What do you need to uphold your boundaries with yourself?

_____

_____

_____

When was a time that you crossed a boundary of your own?

_____

_____

_____

How did you notice that you crossed your own boundary?

_____

_____

_____

What have you done to enhance this boundary since?

_____

_____

_____

Interpersonal boundaries are the limitations set in social scenarios in order to foster mutual respect. You respect others by seeing and abiding by their interpersonal boundaries. You respect yourself by creating clear boundaries with others and enforcing them as needed.

What are some examples of interpersonal boundaries you currently have?

_____

_____

_____

What is an example of a time in which you crossed someone's boundary?

_____

_____

_____

How did you know you crossed a boundary?

_____

_____

_____

What has changed since this event?

_____

_____

_____

How do you know when someone has crossed your boundary?

_____

_____

_____

What emotions arise when someone crosses one of your boundaries?

_____

_____

_____

How do you react when someone crosses one of your boundaries?

_____

_____

_____

How can you improve your boundaries with others?

_____

_____

_____

BOUNDARY BOXES

Boundaries are broad. In order to better understand and uphold your boundaries, it is helpful to be familiar with the different domains of your boundaries, and how they may be similar or different. Common subsections of boundaries are emotional, physical, social, intellectual, sexual, material, time-related, and behavioral. Your domains may include these and others.

Place your current boundaries in the appropriate boxes below. In reflecting on your boundary boxes, you may realize that you are missing boundaries in an area that is important for you to develop. You can use the examples from the previous pages or honor your individuality by highlighting an additional domain that is important to you.

THE MANY HATS WE WEAR

We all wear many hats in our lives. The boundaries you need and establish may vary from role to role. When we connect to who we are, including our personal mission and core values, it is possible that some boundaries are a consistent thread in our hats. However, it is important to note that different situations and contexts may warrant a slight change in boundaries. This does not mean that you are being inconsistent with who you are; instead, it means that you are aware that context will vary throughout your life. It is unlikely you would wear a hard hat to a baseball game or a top hat to the beach. Matching roles and contexts help us to know what types of boundaries are appropriate.

Think about the different hats you wear. To start, there is a specific hat for the boundaries you have with yourself. It may be helpful to think about your overall cultural identity as well (see Cultural Exploration, page 26). It is likely that your boundaries may differ between close loved ones, neighbors, colleagues, and strangers.

Use the space below to highlight your various hats. You can use the surrounding space to note how your boundaries may vary or remain consistent.

BOUNDARY RANGES

Boundaries tend to range from rigid to open. In some contexts, flexible boundaries are useful, whereas in others, firm boundaries are needed. However, people tend to be generally rigid or open.

Review the following chart, and check the traits that relate to you. Be sure to consider your own view, as well as feedback that you have been given throughout your life.

Domains and Their Traits

RIGID	FLEXIBLE	OPEN
❏ Protect your personal information	❏ Be aware of who you are	❏ Overshare your personal information
❏ Avoid connection	❏ Value opinions of others	❏ Connect easily
❏ Rarely ask for help	❏ Consider feedback	❏ Value opinions of others over your own
❏ Detach	❏ Recognize when a boundary is crossed	
❏ Withdraw	❏ Know the need to shift boundaries in accordance with context	❏ Tolerate disrespect
❏ Isolate		❏ Involve yourself in matters beyond yourself
❏ Reject others	❏ Respect yourself	❏ Prioritize others over yourself

How does your flexibility vary in terms of your boundary boxes (see page 129)?

_____

_____

_____

_____

What can you do improve healthy boundaries?

_____

_____

_____

_____

BOUNDARY LEVELS

By now you know that there are many variables to consider in order to create boundaries that affirm your self-respect. Your boundaries may vary by context, environment, and domain. Using what you have learned, think about the different people in your life, including yourself and strangers.

Whom have you established mutual and healthy boundaries with?

_____

_____

_____

_____

Who has established clear boundaries with you but needs to hear your own?

_____

_____

_____

_____

Whom have you established your own boundaries with but need to learn the boundaries of in turn?

_____

_____

_____

Whom do you need to establish boundaries with overall?

_____

_____

_____

What do you need in order to establish helpful boundaries in the future?

_____

_____

_____

BOUNDARY CIRCLES

These concentric circles represent the different levels of your boundaries. The outer circle is likely to include boundaries that are often consistent from person to person across a variety of contexts. This area often has firm boundaries that protect your self-respect regardless of who you are interacting with, including yourself. As you move inward, the gradation changes based on what is appropriate for different scenarios.

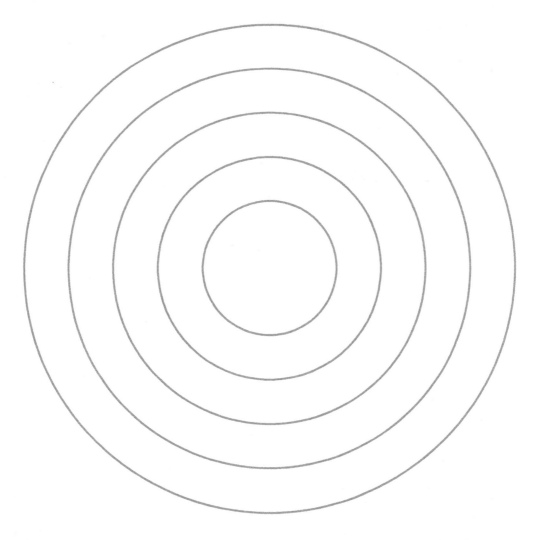

For example, if you strongly value honesty, an outer-layer boundary may be to have a zero-tolerance policy for lying. You may try to catch yourself on the little lies you tell yourself, such as your patterns of unhelpful thinking or the white lies you tell others. Additionally, it may be important to you to hold others accountable when they disrespect you with deceit.

An inner circle may be a boundary that you have with a close loved one. When considering intimacy, your physical, emotional, and sexual boundaries are different with a partner versus a stranger, friend, or colleague. However, it is important to know that while you may let a partner through the gate, it is still essential that a gate exists. For example, in terms of a sexual boundary, consent is still essential but may vary in comparison to consent with an acquaintance.

- Explore what your boundaries look like at these different levels.

- What boundaries do you have at each level?

- What boundaries could you benefit from implementing at each level?

- How do your boundaries change from level to level?

YOUR REMOTE CONTROL

Noticing if your boundaries are being respected or disregarded requires active awareness. To help you gauge, use your inner control system. When your boundaries are respected, you can continue to press play as usual. Sometimes, you need just a brief moment to pause. At other times, you may need to rewind in order to reflect and review the situation. There may also be times in which you need to stop altogether in order to remove yourself from the situation.

How do you know when to use each button?

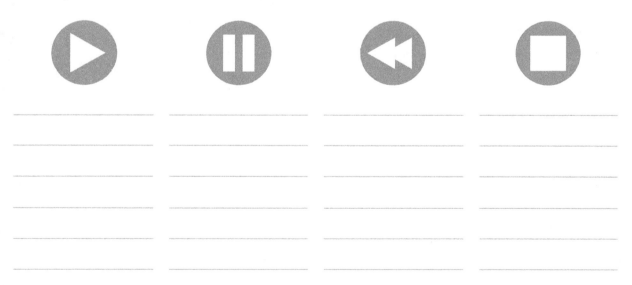

_____   _____   _____   _____

_____   _____   _____   _____

_____   _____   _____   _____

_____   _____   _____   _____

_____   _____   _____   _____

Taking the time to pause or stop is an act of self-love. Advocating for a moment to reassess, reconnect with your core values, and proceed accordingly shows a strong sense of self-respect. Having a plan to help you pause or stop when needed is a proactive way to stand up for who you are and what you believe in.

What do you need when you're in a situation in which you need to pause?

_____

_____

_____

_____

What do you need when you're in a situation in which you need to stop?

_____

_____

_____

_____

ASSERTIVENESS

Assertiveness is a self-loving quality in which you recognize your worth and advocate for yourself. It is a skill that allows you to confidently and respectfully affirm your needs without crossing the fine line into aggressiveness. The ability to be assertive can be improved over time, even in children.

Assertiveness comes with many benefits. It is associated with improvements in mental health, happiness, self-esteem, autonomy, self-acceptance, and personal growth. The benefits of assertiveness are not limited to you, as assertiveness is not selfish. When you are assertive the individuals you interact with are also fortunate to experience respectful and cooperative communication.

Give an example of a time that you needed to practice assertiveness:

_____

_____

_____

_____

What qualities do you have that help you to be assertive?

_____

_____

_____

_____

What opportunities for growth do you have in terms of your assertiveness?

_____

_____

_____

TESTING BOUNDARIES

A key way to practice assertiveness is by clearly conveying and upholding your boundaries with others. When they know your boundaries, they can avoid crossing them. By being assertive, you also help to illuminate your boundaries for individuals uncertain of your personal parameters. Finally, assertiveness can be practical in helping you to enforce your boundaries when crossed and learn how to improve that boundary in the future.

Think of a time when someone crossed your boundary. Place an X on the scale from passive to aggressive to represent how you reacted at that time. Place a star to represent the how you would have liked to react at that time.

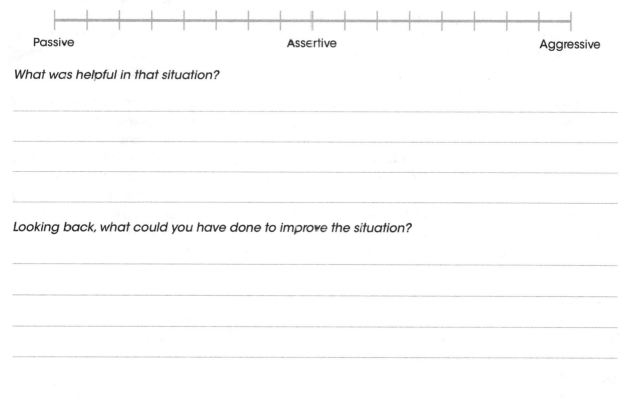

Passive   Assertive   Aggressive

What was helpful in that situation?

_____

_____

_____

_____

Looking back, what could you have done to improve the situation?

_____

_____

_____

_____

TIPS TO BUILD BETTER BOUNDARIES

When you find yourself in a situation in which your boundaries are tested, it is critical to highlight your parameters in order to treat yourself with the dignity that you deserve. However, it can be difficult to manage the careful balance between being passive and aggressive. The six simple tips that follow can help you to practice assertiveness when your boundaries are being tested.

1. Be prepared. When your boundaries are tested, it is important to avoid reacting impulsively. Take the time to pause and step back. Use this time to reflect on the situation and broaden your perspectives. Begin with self-exploration. Remember your worth, reconnect with your values, and remind yourself why your boundaries are important. Then, try to understand your role in the scenario. For example, in considering your responsibilities, you may come to realize that you forgot to make your boundary clear to the other person, but also to yourself. After you thoroughly consider your role in the situation, think of the various perspectives that the person who crossed your boundaries may hold.

After you've come to a thorough understanding of how the boundary was crossed, you can consider how to resolve the concern and move forward. Contemplate the void that needs to be filled. Finally, prepare yourself by deliberating how you can fill the void in an assertive way that upholds your self-respect while maintaining respect for the other person as well.

2. Be clear. Your self-reflection from step 1 provides a foundation for your discussion. Your worth, values, and perspectives are what fuel you to address this potential misunderstanding. In order to clearly convey these important concepts, you must be concise and direct. It can be helpful to brainstorm what you plan to say by writing key components or practicing what you hope to say out load. Be sure to use accurate information to avoid confusion. Although you may have a lot to say, try to pace yourself by providing essential components of your assertiveness in small bits to promote clarity and understanding.

3. Be respectful. Remember, discussing your boundaries is an interpersonal process. Although your self-respect is on the agenda, mutual respect is essential. As you convey your points, it is important to be kind, calm, attentive, and open in the process. If you do not embody these traits it is likely that the assertiveness you wish to convey will be perceived as aggressiveness instead. Although you previously prepared by reflecting on the other person's possible perspectives, in order to maintain balance, you must allow them the space to share their views as well. Try your best to maintain eye contact and convey your sincerity with a collected tone. Actively listen to what they share rather than using the time to selfishly plan your debate. Keep in mind that discussing a boundary that has been tested is not about right or wrong. Instead, it is a self-loving process in which you advocate for your growth and the growth of others around you.

4. Be positive. It can be intimidating to take a stance for your boundaries. Nevertheless, it is a positive, self-loving act. Be optimistic that you have the power to influence the process and can maintain compassion for the person who crossed your boundaries along the way. With that in mind, release responsibility for how the person reacts and take accountability for how you present yourself. Be confident and grounded in your worth, purpose, and present intentions. Although the goal is a productive process resulting in improved boundaries, set your intention that regardless of the outcome, you can be proud that you demonstrated self-respect.

5. Be flexible. Being assertive means protecting your boundaries without stubbornly ignoring the views of the other person. Ideally, both parties show respect, accountability, and responsibility. It is possible that the conversation can prompt you to notice where you could have contributed to the misunderstanding. It is also possible that the discussion may shine a light on a blind spot (see page 29) that you did not previously consider. Be flexible to the other person's needs and consider forgiveness to foster growth.

6. Be persistent. In some instances, the person who tested your boundaries may continue to step over your limits. When this happens, it is important for you to be consistent, firm, and grounded in your self-respect. It is possible that you may need to escalate your intensity to appropriately reinforce your boundary, but this can be a tricky process. You do not want to allow someone to lure you to cross the line into aggressive behavior. You may need to seek help from others. Aid can be as simple as seeking advice; however, depending on the situation, you may need to seek professional help (e.g., police, mental health therapist, attorney).

HEALTHY RELATIONSHIPS

Healthy relationships can promote your self-respect. Positive people can help you to see your worth, even in times that you may not. They can assist you in creating your boundaries, and they can also show you your boundaries can be acknowledged. Furthermore, when you are having trouble forming or enforcing your limits, you can look to those with whom you have healthy relationships as examples of connections based on respect, care, and love.

In the space below, place the initials of the people with whom you have healthy relationships.

Below are several qualities that are commonly found in healthy relationships. Place a star by each quality that is important to you. You can use the blank spaces to add additional qualities that are meaningful to you. Place the initials from the previous page next to each characteristic.

Consideration	Kindness	Care
Trust	Support	Autonomy
Individuality	Understanding	Compromise
Engagement	Effort	Honesty
Respect	Fun	Communication
Equality	Connection	Compassion

What qualities are important to you in a healthy relationship?

_____

_____

_____

_____

Considering the healthy relationships you listed on page 139, what are you missing?

_____

_____

_____

_____

How can you improve your relationships?

_____

_____

_____

_____

IMPROVING MY SUPPORT SYSTEM

"Surround yourself with only people who are going to lift you higher."
—Oprah Winfrey

The relationships you have combine to create your support system. This can include the connections you have at home, work, school, in community groups, or even online. When your support system consists of healthy relationships, it can help to form a barrier against poor self-respect, and it can help to foster enhanced self-respect. A positive sense of support can help to decrease your distress, protect you in times of adversity, and improve your overall quality of life. Your support system begins from the time you are born, and although the system itself fluctuctes throughout the course of your lifetime, its importance remains the same.

REFLECTING ON YOUR SUPPORT SYSTEM

Take a moment to consider the domains of your personal wellness. Do you have healthy relationships to foster each essential aspect?

1. Place your name in the circle on the next page. Use the spokes to represent each of your wellness domains (see page 53). Create additional lines as needed. From each branch, place the names of the people who presently provide support for that aspect of your wellness and help you to maintain balance.

2. Next, consider if there is someone with whom you have a healthy relationship that you have not previously considered to be a part of your support system. Could this person help inspire or encourage you to fulfill any of your wellness domains? If so, place their name with a question mark in the corresponding area.

3. Finally, consider anyone who is unsupportive in your life, specifically someone who is a poor influence on your wellness. Place that person's name in the corresponding area with a strikethrough line over it.

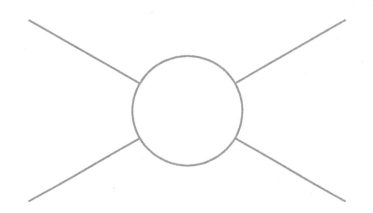

What comes up for you as you reflect on your support system?

_____

_____

_____

_____

_____

_____

FORGIVENESS

"The only thing evil can't stand is forgiveness."
—Fred Rogers

The struggle to forgive is a common obstacle in self-kindness. Believing that you have done something wrong can keep you stuck in the past. This may include things that you regret once saying, doing, or failing to follow through with. Feelings of shame can quickly spiral into sentiments of inferiority and inadequacy, and can hinder your self-love. In order to move forward, you must learn to forgive. Forgiveness is not to be confused with condoning, ignoring, minimizing, or supporting, but simply a promise to learn and grow.

Previously, you explored the importance of Self-Forgiveness (see page 112) in order to improve your self-kindness. However, forgiveness is often an interpersonal process in which you need to apologize or provide forgiveness to others so they can let go of the past as well.

APOLOGIES

When humbly seeking genuine forgiveness it is important to offer an apology, take accountability, and assert your plans for the future. Reflect on apologies you may need to provide to others in order to move forward. Place those examples in the space below.

Choose an example from above and follow the prompts below.

I am sorry that...

_____

_____

I own that I...

_____

_____

In the future I plan to...

_____

_____

I hope...

_____

_____

Reflect on apologies you have waited for, which have caused you to be tethered to the past. Place these examples in the space below.

Although it may be easier to let go after someone offers you an apology, you are able to relinquish the rope on your own. When you are dependent on an apology in order to move forward, you give that person power in your life. Further, being tethered can weigh you down and hold you back from growth. However, you can make the active choice to move forward by releasing the rope. Apology aside, you can progress by honing your self-awareness, reflecting on learned lessons, and living a life that aligns with your mission.

What lessons can you learn from the items above?

_____

_____

_____

* * *

Self-respect begins with your recognition of your worth and is seen by how you honor your worth. It is not entitlement or aggression, but the realization that you are just as deserving of dignity as anyone else. In this chapter you were able to connect with yourself by bringing awareness to the values you wish to embody in this lifetime. To live life filled with integrity, you must create boundaries to allow you to maintain a connection with your ethical code. Through the many roles that you fulfill, your respect can shine through your ability to connect to who you are, in addition to humble acts such as attuning to your self-awareness, fostering forgiveness, and maintaining balance.

SELF-RESPECT REFLECTION

CHAPTER 8

SELF-GROWTH

No one is perfect, and no one will ever be perfect. Additionally, change is inevitable. With time, you change, and the world around you transforms as well. You previously learned that embracing imperfection is an essential component of self-love (page 110). When acknowledging this and pairing it with acceptance of change, you can embrace the notion that there will always be room for growth. When you accept that there isn't a finish line, self-love becomes a process in which you are continually seeking opportunities to learn, love, and thrive. Hence, it is a self-loving practice to recognize where you may have an opportunity to learn, improve, and strive to be the best version of you that you can be.

In the lifelong process of self-growth, you are constantly honing and improving your knowledge of where you are and where you wish you be. You seek to illuminate your blind spots, welcome opportunities for growth, and achieve congruence (page 124) between your ideal self and your true self. Beginning with a reflection of the discrepancy at hand, self-growth also encompasses the steps you take toward your goal as you learn along the way. Additionally, self-growth includes being cognizant of obstacles that may hinder your progression (see Obstacles on page 11), and the methods you take to triumph over those hurdles. In times in which you experience a setback, self-growth also includes the power you evoke to propel yourself forward once again (see Setback Slingshot, page 108).

Your personal growth goals represent where you desire to be in the future. Whether you recognize it or not, they are a part of your everyday life. You also may not realize that you are striving for multiple goals at a time because we are naturally inclined to strive toward self-improvement. When you bring your instinctively goal-oriented process into your awareness, you strengthen your personal growth initiative. Personal growth initiative encompasses the intention and active efforts placed toward goal-achievement. When you heighten your connection to your goals, you can promote self-regulation and improve your functioning as you begin living in accordance with your values. Moreover, achieving progression goals helps to boost your mood and improve your overall well-being.

Counseling psychologist Dr. Kenneth Nowack highlights that initiating new behaviors is often difficult. In order to transition from goal-setting to goal-flourishing, it is essential to follow a process that includes reflection, highlighting strengths, identifying goals, fostering motivation and encouragement, social support, relapse prevention, and evaluation. It is helpful to create a thorough plan with a realistic overview, methods to support change, and strategies to account for setbacks along the way. In order to benefit from the self-loving process of self-growth you need awareness, kindness, and respect along the way.

As you reflect on where you are now, what goals do you have for the future? For this reflection, it may be helpful to jump back to Room for Growth (page 106), The Gracious Gap (page 107), and/or My Personal Qualities (page 75).

HOPES AND DREAMS

"The future belongs to those who believe in the beauty of their dreams."
—Franklin D. Roosevelt

Your self-growth is a personal process. Hence, it is essential to hone your self-awareness and use self-exploration throughout the process. To begin, it can be helpful to connect with who you are. Revisit My Mission Statement (page 42), Values (page 118), and Personal Commandments (page 123).

While connecting with your true self, consider where you are and where you would like to be. Look into the future. What are your hopes and dreams?

If you're having trouble thinking about your hopes and dreams, it may be helpful to revisit the Independent Interview (page 39) to help you self-reflect.

VISION BOARD

When considering your personal growth, it can be helpful to use visuals. Images can inspire and help us illuminate elements that we cannot fully describe with words. Considering where you wish to be in your future, create a small vision board below. Add images that align with your hopes and dreams. The pictures you choose to use may be printed; however, you can create your own doodles as well. Feel free to add powerful words or phrases to formulate your future vision.

For this activity, music can help you to get into a creative zone. Previously you created a Positive Playlist (page 96) with songs that you connect to and that make you happy. You may benefit from using that playlist while you search for and select images to create your vision board. When you use your creativity in this task, you may notice that your expression cannot be confined to the space below. In this case, you can use the area below to brainstorm and create a larger separate vision board to encompass your hopes for the future.

What was it like to create your vision board?

_____

_____

_____

What elements from your vision board stand out for you?

_____

_____

_____

When creating your board, did any negative thinking patterns arise? If so, note them here and practice challenging those negative thoughts.

_____

_____

_____

Consider the concept of congruence. Does your vision board align with your core values?

_____

_____

_____

What strengths do you have to achieve the hopes and dreams encapsulated on your board?

_____

_____

_____

Considering your vision board, where do you believe you have room for growth?

_____

_____

_____

Provide some examples of positive self-talk statements (e.g., affirmations, motivational messages) that you can use to practice self-kindness as you pursue your vision board.

_____

_____

_____

VISUALIZATION

In addition to thinking about where you wish to be, an empowering practice can be to visualize yourself as you wish to be in the future. For example, instead of merely thinking, "one day I would like to own a home," take it one step further by envisioning what this would look like. In this given scenario, what would it look like leading up to having your own home? What would it look like on the first day you step into your own home? When you open the door and cross the threshold, what would you see?

Choose one of your future dreams. Set a timer for one minute. Close your eyes and immerse yourself in that given visual. When your time is up, use the space below to reflect.

You can repeat this activity to help you take your brainstorming and empowerment to another level. When you continue, you may choose to further the same dream, or you may select a different aspiration. As you delve further, you may benefit from increasing the time allotted and depth of reflection as well.

SETTING SELF-LOVING GOALS

At first, setting goals can seem like an intimidating process. Infused with self-love, it can be an enjoyable process instead. The main difference pertains to your perspective in the process. With self-love, your goals are thoroughly considered. You conscientiously create goals that are congruent with who you are and, hence, you are naturally motivated and believe in your ability to achieve your aspirations. As a self-loving process, the journey to goal-attainment is just as important as achieving the goal itself. You craft considerate plans to achieve each aim, including critical steps along the way, support to aid in your progress, and strategies to face your obstacles.

Think about how you have set goals in the past.

What self-love elements have you included in previous goal processes?

_____

_____

_____

What self-love elements do you intend to include in your future goal processes?

_____

_____

_____

SMART GOALS

"It does not do to dwell on dreams and forget to live."
—Albus Dumbledore, *Harry Potter and the Sorcerer's Stone*

Uncertainty pertaining to goals can cause psychological distress. Furthermore, researchers Joanne M. Dickson and Nicholas J. Moberly found that people who are depressed create goals differently. The difference is not that they create fewer goals; instead, their goals tend to be more abstract. When you're setting goals, take adequate time to perform a thorough evaluation, establish concrete goals, and clarify how goals can be achieved. In order to do so, it can be helpful to assure that your goals are SMART.

Specific: Does your goal have precise details?

Measurable: Do you have clear methods to help you track progress?

Attainable: Is it plausible for you to achieve this goal?

Relevant: Does your goal connect to who you are?

Timely: Does the goal have a realistic and flexible timeline?

Example: For the next month, I will use my gratitude journal at least once per day for at least five days each week.

CREATE SMART GOALS

You have had many opportunities to reflect on potential personal growth goals. Now, you will have the opportunity to transform those hopes and dreams into SMART goals. To begin, practice creating SMART goals based on your wellness domains and aspirations. Reflect on the gap between your current wellness wheel (page 55) and your future wellness wheel (page 57). Consider the plans you created to promote self-love (see My Wellness Plan on page 59). Use the template to help you create at least one SMART goal per dimension.

GOAL	S	M	A	R	T
1					
2					
3					
4					

SHORT-TERM AND LONG-TERM GOALS

"You can't cross the sea merely by standing and staring at the water."
—Rabindranath Tagore

It is common to become overwhelmed when considering long-term goals. The time between then and now can cause you to second-guess your dreams. Nevertheless, long-term goals are beneficial as they give you sufficient time to achieve your goal. Furthermore, if things do not go to plan, long-term goals allow you the flexibility to easily practice self-loving values such as patience and kindness. On the other hand, we tend to be more motivated to achieve short-term goals, as they seem more plausible. You can benefit from using a combination of long-term and short-term goals. Long-term goals can help you highlight your future aspirations. Short-term goals can be crafted to help you achieve milestones along the way to making your long-term dreams come true.

Use the space below to brainstorm your future goals.

After brainstorming, create as many long-term personal growth goals as you'd like. Be sure to use the SMART format. Use the pyramid strategy to create short-term building blocks in subsequent layers to help you achieve your dream.

Long-Term Goal

Short-Term Goal 3

Short-Term Goal 2

Short-Term Goal 1

30-DAY SELF-LOVE CHALLENGE

The pursuit of self-growth is a healthy challenge. Planning and consistency are two key elements to help you along your journey. Creating a personalized challenge can help you consider both short and long-term aspirations while creating healthy habits. For example, a 30-day challenge can include your mini-goals that combine to help you achieve your larger goal by the end of the 30 days.

For this task, your SMART goal is to increase your self-love by practicing a self-loving task at least one time per day for 30 days.

Consider the seven segments of self-love (see page 14). To maintain balance, you may wish to divide each section between four days and leave two days flexible to fulfill the area you need the most on that day. You could also focus on the areas you believe you need the most. For example, you may see the most room for growth in the areas of self-esteem and self-kindness. In this situation, you could split the challenge by practicing them on alternating days. Finally, you may opt to focus on one domain. If you choose this option, you can benefit from taking small steps per day to incrementally work toward improving the selected aspect of self-love.

What method(s) have you selected and why?

30-DAY CHALLENGE

Tips:

- Start small, beginning with tasks in which you have high self-efficacy.

- Try to increase the intensity as the challenge progresses.

- Include breaks as needed. After all, a part of self-love is patience and listening to your needs.

- Place this challenge somewhere you can see it, and practice accountability.

1	2	3	4	5
6	7	8	9	10
11	12	13	14	15
16	17	18	19	20
21	22	23	24	25
26	27	28	29	30

SELF-GROWTH CHALLENGE

Now that you have had the opportunity to create a self-love challenge, you can practice applying this method to one of your self-growth aspirations. Select a short-term goal that you can improve in 30 days. You do not have to select a goal that you will fully accomplish in this time frame; however, choose a goal that you can make a substantial change in within 30 days.

SMART Goal: _____

1	2	3	4	5
6	7	8	9	10
11	12	13	14	15
16	17	18	19	20
21	22	23	24	25
26	27	28	29	30

TO-DO LIST

To-do lists can be a helpful resource to help you track the key steps you need to take in order to grow. While long-term to-do lists are useful, short-term to-do lists are particularly practical in helping you to sleep better at night. A self-loving to-do list incorporates your essential tasks while also allowing you to practice self-care, kindness, and respect.

To empower your personal growth, it can be helpful to include self-love elements such as Motivational Messages (page 94), Affirmations (page 95), Encouragers (page 102), and Nice Notes (page 100).

Start small by creating a to-do list with five tasks for tomorrow. Use the space within the shapes to write down tasks that align with either of your 30-day challenges. For example, if you had planned a trip in your self-love challenge, a task for tomorrow may be to brainstorm locations. Feel free to add more as needed.

MY SELF-GROWTH MAP

Now that you have an idea of your future dreams and have clarified some short- and long-term goals, it's time to put it all together in a self-growth map. Doing so will allow you to set your goals in order. You will be able to consider what helps you to fuel your tank, and what helps you in your journey. You will also be able to take a realistic look at the obstacles that you may face in your path. Your heightened awareness can help you improve your conscientiousness, reconnect to your values, and prioritize your goals accordingly. Draw the map in the blank space below.

1. *Select one long-term personal growth goal.*

2. *Draw your path to your goal. Remember, straight paths are rather unlikely.*

3. *Include roadblocks and hurdles you may encounter (see Roadblocks to Self-Love, page 13).*

4. *Include supports that may help you, such as signs of encouragement (see Encouragers, page 102).*

5. *Include premature exits that are likely to tempt you to detour from your goal.*

Self-Growth Map Reflections

1. What goal have you selected?

_____

_____

2. How does this goal relate to your self-love journey?

_____

_____

3. Where are you presently with this goal?

_____

_____

4. How far have you come with this goal?

_____

_____

5. What roadblocks do you anticipate in your path?

_____

_____

6. How do you plan to account for your roadblocks?

_____

_____

7. What sources of support will you have in your path?

_____

_____

8. How will you know when to seek support?

_____

_____

9. How will you know when you are tempted to abandon your path?

_____

_____

10. How will you handle the times you are tempted to abandon your path?

_____

_____

RECOGNIZING OBSTACLES

"When we are no longer able to change a situation,
we are challenged to change ourselves."
—Viktor E. Frankl

Obstacles are to be expected on your journey. You have learned about several potential hindrances, such as blind spots, incongruence, poor wellness or boundaries, negative thinking, and lack of self-patience and forgiveness. Other self-destructive obstacles include self-sabotage and learned helplessness.

Self-sabotage is a form of intrapersonal resistance that can bar your growth. Within this process, you may minimize the pursuit of your goals and end up holding yourself back. Paired with poor self-esteem and a lack of self-kindness, skepticism pertaining to your ability to achieve your goals causes you to block your own path. A common example of this is when an individual is unwilling to seek help that could be catalyst for progress.

Self-handicapping is a mental strategy in which you create excuses to preserve your self-esteem. The excuses provide a justification for your lack of achievement, and, in turn, allow you to avoid direct accountability for your actions, or lack thereof. Self-handicapping provides the opportunity to externalize blame. For example, you may frame your lateness on the traffic, even if you were already likely to be tardy due to going to bed late and not setting an alarm for the morning. Sometimes it is difficult to discern whether a sincere rationale exists or whether you are personally placing an obstacle in your path.

Learned helplessness evolves from repeated exposure to difficult setbacks. An individual who has experienced multiple difficulties may start to generalize this pattern. As a result, individuals become likely to see their inability even in times in which they are able. For example, consider an individual who wants to lose weight. If this person tried several fad diets and did not see any results, he or she may forfeit their attempts at achieving a healthier body. However, the individual may not be seeing the impact of an underlying health condition, the effects of a mental health diagnosis, or the important role of exercise in weight loss. Nevertheless, the lack of progress may cause this person to lose inspiration and motivation that could affect his or her weight loss journey, and could permeate into personal growth overall.

Consider the obstacles we covered in this workbook. What hurdles are you likely to face in your path?

_____

_____

_____

_____

_____

HANDLING SETBACKS

"Life is like riding a bicycle. To keep your balance, you must keep moving."
—Albert Einstein

When you experience setbacks, you naturally begin to reassess the goal. You may analyze the pros and cons associated with the goal, and whether it is still important to you. Oftentimes, setbacks have a snowball effect. Rather than getting up, dusting off your hands, and moving forward, when tainted by the aftermath of a setback, you may no longer see your goals as doable or desirable. Hence, setbacks can be discouraging and may tempt you to forfeit your future aspirations.

Previously you learned about the likelihood of setbacks as you learn and grow, and the importance of practicing self-kindness as they occur. In addition, it is important to proactively consider your obstacles; you can equip yourself with the tools to handle these hurdles if you encounter them. Think about it this way: If you have a walk in the park planned, a 50 percent chance of rain could be a setback. However, this doesn't mean you can't enjoy your stroll. Perhaps you may grab an umbrella or a raincoat to prepare for the rain and avoid the potential deterrence.

Planning ahead allows you the openness to monitor and adjust to feedback. A continued connection to your self-awareness may also help you to deter setbacks. If you know that lack of sleep will cause you to be groggy at work, for example, then you can intentionally aim for a restful evening prior to a big meeting the next morning. Furthermore, continued setbacks in an area can be used as flags to reconsider your approach. If you realize that simply hopping into bed earlier doesn't equate to improved sleep, then over time, you may use methods to adjust your sleeping routine. Ultimately, you may learn that you achieve ample rest by using an aromatherapy diffuser, turning off your devices, and making a gratitude list before bed.

What setbacks could you face in your path of personal growth?

_____

_____

_____

_____

How will you handle such setbacks?

_____

_____

_____

_____

What type of self-kindness statement could you use for your slingshot if this occurs? See page 108, Setback Slingshot.

_____

_____

_____

_____

STAGES OF CHANGE

"I think goals should never be easy, they should force you to work, even if they are uncomfortable at the time."
—Michael Phelps

A failure to consider how ready you are to make a change can cause you to experience setbacks in self-growth. James Prochaska and Carlo DiClemente's Stages of Change model can help you to understand how to prompt behavioral change. As shown in the stages below, an emphasis is placed on an individual's readiness as an essential factor in progression. Also, Prochaska and DiClemente highlight that growth often occurs in a non-linear fashion, and setbacks are a normal part of the process.

- **Precontemplation:** If you are in precontemplation, you are not even thinking about making the change at hand. You have no intention of changing and it is likely that you do not even recognize that a change may be beneficial.

- **Contemplation:** If you are in contemplation, you are just beginning to think about setting a potential goal to change. You may be uncertain, but sincere consideration is present.

- **Preparation:** If you are in preparation, you are ready, determined, and make the necessary adjustments to mentally prepare yourself to work toward your goal.

- **Action:** If you are in the action stage, you are committed to your goal and are following through with the necessary steps to progress toward your achievement.

- **Maintenance:** If you are in the maintenance stage, you have progressed from a continued action phase, and may have even achieved your goal. At this time your efforts are fostering sustained change.

According to the Stages of Change model, you can recycle, or experience setbacks at any time. However, jumping back on the wagon keeps you on an upward spiral in which you are still progressing toward self-growth.

READY, SET, GO!

Create a key for your self-growth goals. List them below and select a symbol for each.

Place your self-growth symbols near the corresponding stage of change below.

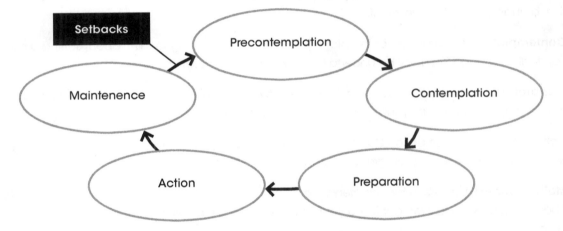

Use this section for an open-ended reflection.

_____

_____

_____

_____

_____

_____

THE SILVER LINING SURROUNDING CHALLENGES

"We may encounter many defeats but we must not be defeated."
—Maya Angelou

Challenges are opportunities for you to triumph. We often think about difficult times negatively; however, if you look close enough, a positive perspective will highlight the silver lining. You may think that the absence of challenge is your ideal, but positive psychologist Mihaly Csikszentmihályi posits that without challenge we may actually be quite apathetic and bored. Furthermore, when we are equipped for the difficult task at hand, we experience flow. Also referred to as being in the zone, flow is a positive mental state in which you enjoy, and are deeply immersed in, the difficult task at hand. Even in the times we may not be fully prepared for the task, our reaction to the challenge can show the positive trait of resilience. Resilience is the ability to persevere, regardless of hindrances and defeats. Finally, enduring a stressor can provoke personal growth that you may not have experienced otherwise.

APPLYING A SILVER LINING

Revisit the activities you explored in My Self-Efficacy (page 81) and Setback Slingshot (page 108). List those activities around the box and draw an arrow to the appropriate section where they belong.

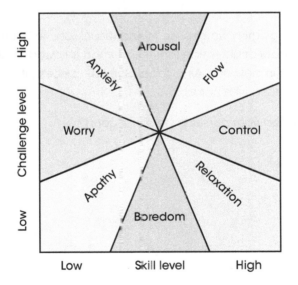

What do you need in order to achieve flow while pursuing your personal growth goals?

_____

_____

_____

_____

Apply a silver-lining to the potential setbacks you may experience on your self-growth journey.

_____

_____

_____

_____

LEARNED LESSONS

"I have not failed. I've just found 10,000 ways that won't work."
—Thomas A. Edison

Setbacks can be empowering when we choose to find the lessons within them. For example, multiple unsuccessful attempts at a goal could mean that the method is flawed, the goal is not congruent with who you are, or many things in between. As a self-exploratory process, it can be beneficial to find the lessons in the times you are faced with hardship.

What lessons have you learned from pursuing personal goals?

_____

_____

_____

_____

_____

Use this space to reflect on lessons that you learned in pursuit of your new personal growth goals.

MY SUPPORT SYSTEM

Your social support system (see page 141 and the activity below) can be a powerful resource in your self-growth process. Individuals who are close to you can help to keep you accountable, provide feedback, remind you to be kind to yourself, and serve as motivators. In order to be supportive, the individuals within your sphere do not need to provide direct guidance. Just having their encouragement as you foster autonomy in walking your own path is beneficial. As you work through setbacks, your social support system can help you. If you know individuals who are working toward their own goals, regardless of obstacles they may face, this can set an inspiring example to help you see your journey as manageable.

WHO SUPPORTS YOUR SELF-GROWTH?

Make a column for each personal growth goal you created earlier in this chapter. In each section, list the people who you know you can count on to support you in the given goal. You can list someone in more than one column, if applicable.

You have completed three support system activities. Have you noticed any changes in the process?

_____

_____

_____

How do you know when you can count on someone to support your self-growth?

_____

_____

_____

Did you list someone in several columns?

_____

_____

_____

Did you list anyone in only one column?

_____

_____

_____

It is healthy for support to be symbiotic. Individuals who support you may benefit from your support as well. Support is a form of love. Providing support for others honors their worth, just as you wish for them to honor yours. When you care for others through the conduit of support, the love that you give can come right back to you and can benefit your self-loving practice.

Use the chart below to flip your perspective on social support. List each person who appeared in your support system. Then, delve into how you know they support you, how they need support, and how you provide support for them as well.

Name	__ supports me by ..	__ needs support for...	I provide __ with support by...

GIVING AND GROWING

"Be the change that you wish to see in the world."
—Mahatma Gandhi

Charity is a specific method of support that improves your happiness and promotes self-love. Its benefits include an improvement in well-being, enhancements in life satisfaction, and a reduction in symptoms of mental health impairment, such as depression. When you help others, positive sentiments are evoked that improve your well-being and ability to love yourself and others. While charity tends to have a powerful impact on wellness when you give to people you know, you do not need to limit yourself to those who are in your support system. Choosing to pay it forward by donating or volunteering to causes that are important to you is a way that you can be congruent with your values and help yourself, while helping others in need.

PAYING IT FORWARD

"Peace is our gift to each other."
—Elie Wiesel

Brainstorm ways in which you can be helpful. This can include volunteering, donating, or random acts of kindness. Draw a ticket for each idea in the space below.

CONTINUED LEARNING

"It does not matter how slowly you go as long as you do not stop."
—Confucius

An essential aspect of self-growth is the humble acceptance that learning is a continuous process. Obstacles will arise and setbacks are likely. However, your perseverance will allow you to see lessons in such challenges. Additionally, even when you come to the point in your path in which all of the personal goals you set in this chapter have been met, your journey will not be concluded. Be mindful that new paths will surface. As an aspect of self-love, it is helpful to balance acceptance with persistence.

Beyond the goals you crafted, in which areas do you believe you would like to improve your learning?

_____

_____

_____

_____

_____

How will you keep an open mind to new goals that arise?

_____

_____

_____

_____

_____

Use this space to jot down new paths for growth as they arise:

_____

_____

_____

_____

_____

MENTAL HEALTH COUNSELING

In your self-love journey you explore the depths of who you are in order to understand how to best love yourself. In the process, you may notice signs of mental health distress impeding your progress. Just as you are prone to physical problems throughout your lifetime, it is probable that you will endure mental health concerns as well.

The World Health Organization asserts that mental and substance concerns are the leading cause of disability worldwide. Mental Health America highlights that one in five Americans has a mental health condition. However, mental health problems tend to be underreported as many individuals may not even know they are experiencing a mental health problem and may not seek help. And regardless of the diagnosis, mental health symptoms alone are distressing and warrant help.

According to the Mental Health Foundation, almost three in four people report feeling so stressed that they have been unable to cope, a critical aspect in self-care and self-love. While self-love is entirely possible to achieve despite a mental health diagnosis, poor mental hygiene can serve as an obstacle in your personal growth. Nevertheless, self-love can be a useful element to improve your mental health. However, depending on the level of concern, you may need to seek the help of a trained mental health professional to assist you in your healing.

Here are signs of a mental health problem:

- **Mood.** Poor mood can be a sign of a mental health problem. Also, prolonged episodes of negative emotions or drastic changes can be concerning. Examples include excessive fear, consistent sadness, or prolonged irritability.

- **Thoughts.** Long-standing negative thinking can be a symptom of an underlying mental health problem. Additionally, experiencing an increase in confusion or a decrease in the ability to concentrate may be a sign of a mental health problem.

- **Habits.** When dealing with a mental health problem, an individual may be distracted and common daily habits and preferences may shift. For example, a person may experience difficulty sleeping or eating. These changes may cause a person to experience a decrease in productivity that can affect key dimensions of life, such as school, work, or family.

- **Disconnecting.** Individuals with a mental health concern may experience a disinterest in domains that previously prompted joy. For example, they may avoid positive coping and disconnect from loved ones. Even when trying to engage with others, individuals facing mental unwellness may struggle to connect.

- **Poor coping.** In an attempt to cope, individuals who are suffering with poor mental hygiene may end up turning to maladaptive coping mechanisms such as substance abuse and self-harm.

If you or someone you know needs helps now, you should immediately call the National Suicide Prevention Lifeline at 1-800-273-8255, or call 911.

Do you have any of the signs of a mental health problem?

_____

_____

_____

_____

_____

Mental hygiene is just as important as physical hygiene. How do you tend to your mental hygiene?

_____

_____

_____

_____

_____

* * *

It is a self-loving practice to recognize your worth and potential. When you embrace the endless possibilities within the realm of learning, you unlock opportunities to flourish. You are then able to honor your worth, strive to achieve your own aspirations, and become the best version of yourself. In this chapter you gained the clarity to see your hopes and dreams, foreseeable challenges, and methods to support you beyond your obstacles. With self-love, you are now able to visualize your goals, strategize your path, and courageously embark on your journey.

SELF-GROWTH REFLECTION

BIBLIOGRAPHY

Aalbers, S., Fusar-Poli, L., Freeman, R. E. et al. "Music Therapy for Depression." *Cochrane Database of Systematic Reviews* 11 (2017). doi: 10.1002/14651858.CD004517.pub3.

Action for Happiness. "Self-Acceptance Could Be the Key to a Happier Life." March 2014. http://www.actionforhappiness.org/news/self-acceptance-could-be-the-key-to-a-happier-life.

Allen, T. J. and Sherman, J. W. "Ego Threat and Intergroup Bias: A Test of Motivated-Activation versus Self-Regulatory Accounts." *Psychological Science* 22, no. 3 (2011). doi: 10.1177/0956797611399291.

Andrew, B. S. "*Self-Respect and Loving Others*." In Sex, Love, and Friendship: Studies of the Society for the Philosophy of Friendship and Love: 1993–2003, edited by A. L. McEvoy, 191–96. New York: Rodophi, 2011.

Ashforth, B. E., Kreiner, G. E., & Fugate, M. "All in a Day's Work: Boundaries and Micro Role Transitions." *Academy of Management Review* 25, no. 3 (2000): 472–91. doi: 10.2307/259305.

Avşar, F. and Ayaz, A. S. "The Effectiveness of Assertiveness Training for School-Aged Children on Bullying and Assertiveness Level." *Journal of Pediatric Nursing* 36 (2017): 186–90. doi: 10.1016/j.pedr.2017.06.020.

Ayala, E. E., Omorodion, A. M., Nmecha, D., et al. "What Do Medical Students Do for Self-Care? A Student-Centered Approach to Well-Being." *Teaching & Learning in Medicine* 29, no. 3 (2017): 237–46. doi: 10.1080/10401334.2016.1271334.

Ayduk, O. and Kross, E. "From a Distance: Implications of Spontaneous Self-Distancing for Adaptive Self-Reflection." *Journal of Personality and Social Psychology* 98, no. 5 (2010): 809–29. doi: 10.1037/a0019205.

Baker, T. E. "Burnout." In *Encyclopedia of Trauma: An Interdisciplinary Guide*, edited by C. R. Figley. Thousand Oaks, CA: Sage Publications, 2012.

Beck, A. T. *Depression; Causes and Treatment*. Philadelphia: University of Pennsylvania Press, 1972.

Berglas, S. and Jones, E. E. "Drug Choice as a Self-Handicapping Strategy in Response to Noncontingent Success." *Journal of Personality and Social Psychology* 36, no. 4 *(1978)*: 405–17. doi: 10.1037/0022-3514.36.4.405.

Bruhn, A. L., Fernando, J., McDaniel, S. et al. "Putting Behavioral Goal-Setting Research into Practice." *Beyond Behavior* 26, no. 2 (2017): 66–73. doi: 10.1177/1074295617711208.

Bucholz, E. M., Strait, K. M., Dreyer, R. P. et al. "Effect of Low Perceived Social Support on Health Outcomes in Young Patients with Acute Myocardial Infarction." *Journal of the American Heart Association* 3, no. 5 (2014): e001252. doi: 10.1161/JAHA.114.001252.

Calhoun, L. G. and Tedeschi, R. G, eds. *The Handbook of Posttraumatic Growth: Research and Practice*. New York: Routledge, 2004.

Carpenter, T. P., Carlisle, R.D., Tsang, J. "Tipping the Scales: Conciliatory Behavior and the Morality of Self-Forgiveness." *Journal of Positive Psychology* 9, no. 5 (2014): 389–401. doi: 10.1080/17439760.2014.910823.

Cavanaugh, L. A., Bettman, J. R., Luce, M.F. "Feeling Love and Doing More for Distant Others: Specific Positive Emotions Differentially Affect Prosocial Consumption." *Journal of Marketing Research* 52, no. 5 (2015): 657–73. doi: 10.1509/jmr.10.0219.

Centers for Disease Control and Prevention. "Choose Respect Community Action Kit: Helping Preteens and Teens Build Healthy Relationships." 2005. http://www.aldine.k12.tx.us/cms/file_process/download.cfm?docID=BED9BF514B2EAD07.

Chiaburu, D. S. and Marinova, S. V. "What Predicts Skill Transfer? An Exploratory Study of Goal Orientation, Training Self-Efficacy and Organizational Supports." *International Journal of Training and Development* 9, no. 2 (2005): 110–23. doi: 10.1111/j.1468-2419.2005.00225.x.

Choi, A. N., Lee, M. S., Lee, J. S. "Group Music Intervention Reduces Aggression and Improves Self-Esteem in Children with Highly Aggressive Behavior: A Pilot Controlled Trial." *Evidence-Based Complementary and Alternative Medicine* 7, no. 2 (2010): 213–17. doi: 10.1093/ecam/nem182.

Chong Guan, N., Kiah Tian, L., Seng Beng, T. et al. "The Effect of 5 Minutes of Mindful Breathing to the Perception of Distress and Physiological Responses in Palliative Care Cancer Patients: A Randomized Controlled Study." *Journal of Palliative Medicine* 19, no. 9 (2016): 917–24. doi: 10.1089/jpm.2016.0046.

Colgan, D. D., Christopher, M., Michael, P. et al. "The Body Scan and Mindful Breathing among Veterans with PTSD: Type of Intervention Moderates the Relationship between Changes in Mindfulness and Post-Treatment Depression." *Mindfulness* 7, no. 2 (2016): 372–83. doi: 10.1007/s12671-015-0453-0.

Connelly, B. S. and Ones, D. S. "An Other Perspective on Personality: Meta-Analytic Integration of Observers' Accuracy and Predictive Validity." *Psychological Bulletin* 136 no. 6 (2010): 1092–22. doi: 10.1037/a0021212.

Crenshaw, K. "Demarginalizing the Intersection of Race and Sex: A Black Feminist Critique of Antidiscrimination Doctrine, Feminist Theory and Antiracist Politics," University of Chicago Legal Forum 1989, no. 1 (1989): 139–67. https://chicagounbound.uchicago.edu/uclf/vol1989/iss1/8.

Csikszentmihályi, M. *Flow: The Psychology of Optimal Experience.* New York: Harper & Row, 1990.

Dalton, A. N. and Spiller, S. A. "Too Much of a Good Thing: The Benefits of Implementation Intentions Depend on the Number of Goals." *Journal of Consumer Research* 39, no. 3 (2012): 600–14. doi: 10.1086/664500.

deFur, K. "Selections from Unequal Partners: Teaching about Power, Consent, and Healthy Relationships." *American Journal of Sexuality Education* 11, no. 2 (2016): 149–59. doi: 10.1080/15546128.2016.1174025.

Derrick, J. L., Gabriel, S. Tippin, B. "Parasocial Relationships and Self-Discrepancies: Faux Relationships Have Benefits for Low Self-Esteem Individuals." *Personal Relationships* 15, no. 2 (2008): 261–80. doi: 10.1111/j.1475-6811.2008.00197.x.

Drick, C. A. "Coming Alive in Presence: The Cornerstone of 21st Century Holistic Nursing." *Beginnings* 37, no. 2 (2017): 12–14.

Drick, C. A. "Maternity Quality Improvement through Nurses' Self-Care." *International Journal of Childbirth Education* 33, no. 2 (2018): 24–28.

Drick, C. A. "Self-Care: A Busy Person's Guide to Finding Time and Balance." *Beginnings* 36, no. 4 (2016): 6–7.

Elvers, P., Fischinger, T., Steffens, J. "Music Listening as Self-Enhancement: Effects of Empowering Music on Momentary Explicit and Implicit Self-Esteem." *Psychology of Music* 46, no. 3 (2017): 307–25. doi: 10.1177/0305735617707354.

Ezzedeen, S. R. and Zikic, J. "Finding Balance amid Boundarylessness: An Interpretive Study of Entrepreneurial Work-Life Balance and Boundary Management." *Journal of Family Issues* 38, no. 11 (2015): 1546–76. doi: 10.1177/0192513X15600731.

Fisher, M. J. and Exline, J. J. "Self-Forgiveness versus Excusing: The Roles of Remorse, Effort, and Acceptance of Responsibility." *Self and Identity* 5, no. 2 (2007): 127–47. doi: 10.1080/15298860600586123.

Ghorbani, N., Watson, P. J., Hargis, M. B. "Integrative Self-Knowledge Scale: Correlations and Incremental Validity of a Cross-Cultural Measure Developed in Iran and the United States." *Journal of Psychology* 142, no. 4 (2008): 395–412. doi: 10.3200/JRPL.142.4.395-412.

Glass, N. and Rose, J. "Enhancing Emotional Well-Being through Self-Care. The Experiences of Community Health Nurses in Australia." *Holistic Nursing Practice* 22, no. 6 (2008): 336–47. doi: 10.1097/01.HNP.0000339345.26500.62.

Gollwitzer, P. M. and Sheeran, P. "Implementation Intentions and Goal Achievement: A Meta-Analysis of Effects and Processes." *Advances in Experimental Social Psychology* 38 (2006): 69 –119. doi: 10.1016/ S0065-2601(06)38002-1.

Griffiths, A., Royse, D., Walker, R. "Stress among Child Protective Service Workers: Self-Reported Health Consequences." *Children and Youth Services Review* 90 (2018): 46–53. doi: 10.1016/j.childyouth.2018.05.011.

Hafenbrack, C., Kinias, Z. Barsade, S. G. "Debiasing the Mind through Meditation: Mindfulness and the Sunk-Cost Bias." *Psychological Science* 25, no. 2 (2013): 369. doi: 10.1177/0956797613503853.

Hamilton, H. R. and DeHart, T. "Drinking to Belong: The Effect of a Friendship Threat and Self-Esteem on College Student Drinking." *Self and Identity* 16, no. 1 (2017): 1–15. doi: 10.1080/15298868.2016.1210539.

Hasannia, S. and Sedghpour, B. S. "The Relationship between Assertiveness and Happiness with Self-Efficacy: Structural Equation Modeling." *Journal of Psychology* 21, no. 1 (2017): 85–100.

Hays, P. A. *Addressing Cultural Complexities in Practice: Assessment, Diagnosis, and Therapy,* 2nd edition. Washington, D. C.: American Psychological Association, 2008.

Helmond, P., Overbeek, G., Brugman, D., et al. "A Meta-Analysis on Cognitive Distortions and Externalizing Problem Behavior." *Criminal Justice and Behavior* 42, no. 3 (2015): 245–62. doi: 10.1177/0093854814552842.

Hill Jones, S. "A Delicate Balance: Self-Care for the Hospice Professional." *Aging Well* 1, no. 2 (2008): 38. http://www.todaysgeriatricmedicine.com/archive/spring08p38.shtml.

Holzel, B. K., Carmody, J., Vangel, M. et al. "Mindfulness Practice Leads to Increases in Regional Brain Gray Matter Density." *Psychiatry Research: Neuroimaging* 19, no.1 (2011): 36–43. doi: 10.1016/j.pscychresns.2010.08.006.

Honneth, A. *The I in We: Studies in the Theory of Recognition.* Cambridge: Polity Press, 2012.

Honneth, A. *The Struggle for Recognition.* Translated by J. R. Anderson. Cambridge: Polity Press, 1995.

Hsu, D. Y., Huang, L., Nordgren, L. F. et al. "The Music of Power: Perceptual and Behavioral Consequences of Powerful Music." *Social Psychological and Personality Science 6, no. 1* (2015): 75–83. doi: 10.1177/1948550614542345.

Inderscience Publishers. "Social Giving Makes Us Happier." Science Daily. August 2013. www.sciencedaily.com/releases/2013/08/130820135034.htm.

Jenkinson, C. E., Dickens, A. P., Jones, K. et al. "Is Volunteering a Public Health Intervention? A Systematic Review and Meta-Analysis of the Health and Survival of Volunteers." *BMC Public Health 13, no. 1* (2013): 773. doi: 10.1186/1471-2458-13-773.

Jones, E. E. and Berglas, S. "Control of Attributions about the Self through Self-Handicapping Strategies: The Appeal of Alcohol and the Role of Underachievement." *Journal of Personality and Social Psychology* 4, no. 2 (1978): 200–6.

Kabat-Zinn, J. *Wherever You Go, There You Are: Mindfulness Meditation in Everyday Life.* New York: Hyperion, 1994.

Kant, I. "Metaphysical Principles of Virtue." In *Ethical Philosophy.* Translated by J. W. Ellington. Indianapolis: Hackett Publishing Co., 1982.

Kernis, M. H., Lakey, C. E., Heppner, W. L. "Secure Versus Fragile High Self-Esteem as a Predictor of Verbal Defensiveness: Converging Findings across Three Different Markers." *Journal of Personality* 76, no. 3 (2008): 477–512. doi: 10.1111/j.1467-6494.2008.00493.x.

Knauper, B., McCollam, A., Rosen-Brown, A. et al. "Fruitful Plans: Adding Targeted Mental Imagery to Implementation Intentions Increases Fruit Consumption." *Psychology and Health* 26, no. 5 (2011): 601–17. doi: 10.1080/08870441003703218.

Koestner, R., Powers, T. A., Milyavskaya, M. et al. "Goal Internalization and Persistence as a Function of Autonomous and Directive Forms of Goal Support." *Journal of Personality* 83, no. 2 (2015): 179–90. doi: 10.1111/jopy.12093.

Kuhn, C. M. and Flanagan, E. M. "Self-Care as a Professional Imperative: Physician Burnout, Depression, and Suicide." *Canadian Journal of Anaesthesia* 64, no. 2 (2017): 158–68. doi: 10.1007/s12630-016-0781-0.

Lee, C. C. and Ali, S. "Intersectionality: Understanding the Complexity of Identity in Counseling across Cultures." In *Multicultural Issues in Counseling: New Approaches to Diversity,* 5th Ed., edited by C. C. Lee, 23–30. Alexandria, VA: American Counseling Association, 2019.

Gallrein, A. B., Carlson, E. N., Holstein, M. et al. "You Spy with Your Little Eye: People Are 'Blind' to Some of the Ways in Which They Are Consensually Seen By Others." *Journal of Research in Personality* 47, no. 5 (2013): 464–71. doi: 10.1016/j.jrp.2013.04.001.

Liu, S. Y., Wrosch, C., Miller, G. E. et al. "Self-Esteem Change and Diurnal Cortisol Secretion in Older Adulthood." *Psychoneuroendocrinology* 41 (2014): 111–20. doi: 10.1016/j.psyneuen.2013.12.010.

Locke, E. A. and Latham, G. P, eds. *New Developments in Goal Setting and Task Performance.* New York: Routledge, 2013.

Luft, J. and Ingham, H. "*The Johari Window, a Graphic Model for Interpersonal Relations.*" Proceedings of the Western Training Laboratory in Group Development. Los Angeles: University of California, Los Angeles (1955).

Ljungberg, A., Denhov, A., Topor, A. "A Balancing Act—How Mental Health Professionals Experience Being Personal in Their Relationships with Service Users." *Issues in Mental Health Nursing* 38, no. 7 (2017): 578–83. doi: 10.1080/01612840.2017.1301603.

Lindwall, M., Hülya Aşçı, F., Palmeira, A. et al. "The Importance of Importance in the Physical Self: Support for the Theoretically Appealing but Empirically Elusive Model of James." *Journal of Personality* 79, no. 2 (2011): 303–34. doi: 10.1111/j.1467-6494.2010.00678.x.

Martin, H. J. "Workplace Climate and Peer Support as Determinants of Training Transfer." *Human Resource Development Quarterly* 21, no. 1 (2010): 87–104. doi: 10.1002/hrdq.20038.

Maslow, A. *Toward a Psychology of Being*, 2nd ed. New York: Van Nostrand, 1968.

Mayer, J. D., Salovey, P., Caruso, D. R. "Emotional Intelligence: Theory, Findings, and Implications." *Psychological Inquiry* 15, no. 3 (2004): 197–215.

Mental Health America. "The State of Mental Health in America," 2018. http://www.mentalhealthamerica.net/issues/state-mental-health-america.

Milyavskaya, M. and Werner, K. M. "Goal Pursuit: Current State of Affairs and Directions for Future Research." *Canadian Psychology* 59, no. 2 (2018): 163–75. doi: 10.1037/cap0000147.

Miranda, D. and Claes, M. "Music Listening, Coping, Peer Affiliation and Depression in Adolescence." *Psychology of Music* 37, no. 2 (2009): 215–33. doi: 10.1177/0305735608097245.

Mitzman, S. F. "Clinically Depressed Adults' Idiographic Goals and Causal Explanations." Clin.Psy.D. thesis, University of Birmingham, 2013. http://etheses.bham.ac.uk/4089.

Moberly, N. J. and Dickson, J. M. "Goal Conflict, Ambivalence and Psychological Distress: Concurrent and Longitudinal Relationships." *Personality and Individual Differences* 129 (2018): 38–42. doi: 10.1016/j.paid.2018.03.008.

Myers, J. E. and Sweeney, T. J. "The Indivisible Self: An Evidence-Based Model of Wellness." *Journal of Individual Psychology* 60, no. 3 (2004): 234–45. http://libres.uncg.edu/ir/uncg/f/J_Myers_Indivisible_2004.pdf.

Neff, K. D., Rude, S. S., Kirkpatrick, K. L. "An Examination of Self-Compassion in Relation to Positive Psychological Functioning and Personality Traits." *Journal of Research in Personality* 41, no. 4 (2007): 908–16. doi: 10.1016/j.jrp.2006.08.002.

Neff, K. D., Hsieh, Y.-P., Dejitterat, K. "Self-Compassion, Achievement Goals, and Coping with Academic Failure." *Self and Identity* 4 *no. 3* (2005): 263–87. doi: 10.1080/13576500444000317.

Neff, K. D. "The Development and Validation of a Scale to Measure Self-Compassion." *Self and Identity* 2, no. 3 (2003): 223–50. doi: 10.1080/15298860309027.

Neff, K. D. and McGehee, P. "Self-Compassion and Psychological Resilience among Adolescents and Young Adults." *Self and Identity* 9, no. 3 (2010): 225–40. doi: 10.1080/15298860902979307.

Neff, K. D. and Germer, C. K. "A Pilot Study and Randomized Controlled Trial of the Mindful Self-Compassion Program." *Journal of Clinical Psychology* 69, no. 1 (2012): 28–44. doi: 10.1002/jclp.21923.

Neff, K. D. "Self-Compassion: An Alternative Conceptualization of a Healthy Attitude toward Oneself." *Self and Identity* 2, no. 2 (2003): 85–101. doi: 10.1080/15298860309032.

Nowack, K. "Facilitating Successful Behavior Change: Beyond Goal Setting to Goal Flourishing." *Consulting Psychology Journal: Practice and Research* 69, no. 3 (2017): 153–171. doi: 10.1037/cpb0000088.

Orehek, E. and Forest, A. L. "When People Serve as Means to Goals: Implications of a Motivational Account of Close Relationships." *Current Directions in Psychological Science* 25, no. 2 (2016): 79 –84. doi: 10.1177/ 0963721415623536.

Parray, W. M. "Impact of Assertiveness Training on the Level of Assertiveness, Self-Esteem, Stress, Psychological Well-Being and Academic Achievement of Adolescents." *Indian Journal of Health and Wellbeing* 8, no. 12 (2017): 1476–80.

Pourjali, F. and Zarnaghash, M. "Relationships between Assertiveness and the Power of Saying No with Mental Health among Undergraduate Students." *Procedia: Social and Behavioral Sciences* 9 (2010): 137–141. doi: 10.1016/j.sbspro.2010.12.126.

Prochaska, J. O., Norcross, J. C., DiClemente, C. C. *Changing for Good: A Revolutionary Six-Stage Program for Overcoming Bad Habits and Moving Your Life Positively Forward*. New York: William Morrow, 1994.

Renger, D. "Believing in One's Equal Rights: Self-Respect as a Predictor of Assertiveness." *Self and Identity* 17, no. 1 (2018): 1–21. doi: 10.1080/15298868.2017.1313307.

Richards, K. C., Campenni, C. E., Muse-Burke, J. L. "Self-Care and Well-Being in Mental Health Professionals: The Mediating Effects of Self-Awareness and Mindfulness." *Journal of Mental Health Counseling* 32, no. 3 (2010): 247–264. doi: 10.17744/ mehc.32.3.0n31v88304423806.

Righetti, F. and Visserman, M. "I Gave Too Much." *Social Psychological and Personality Science 9, no. 4* (2017): 453–60. doi: 10.1177/1948550617707019.

Rippo, M. "Minding the Mind/Body Connection in Moving Beyond Self-Sabotage and Resistance to Change." *Journal of Heart Centered Therapies* 19, no. 2 (2016): 39.

Robitschek, C. "Personal Growth Initiative: The Construct and Its Measure." *Measurement and Evaluation in Counseling and Development* 30, no. 4 (1998): 183–98.

Roelofs, L. I. "Rational Agency without Self-Knowledge: Could 'We' Replace 'I'?" *Dialectica* 71, no. 1 (2017): 3–33. doi: 10.1111/1746-8361.12169.

Rogers, C. *On Becoming a Person*. Boston: Houghton Mifflin, 1961.

Rokach, A. "Caring for Those Who Care for the Dying: Coping with the Demands of Palliative Care Workers." *Palliative and Supportive Care* 3, no. 4 (2005): 325–32. https://www.ncbi.nlm.nih.gov/pubmed/17039988.

Ross, A., Bevans, M., Brooks, A. T. et al. "Nurses and Health-Promoting Behaviors: Knowledge May Not Translate into Self-Care." *AORN Journal* 105, no. 3 (2017): 267–275. doi: 10.1016/j.aorn.2016.12.018.

Rotter, J. B. "Generalized Expectancies for Internal versus External Control of Reinforcement." *Psychological Monographs: General and Applied* 80, no. 1 (1966): 1–28. doi: 10.1037/h0092976.

Ruderman, E. G. "Nurturance and Self-Sabotage: Psychoanalytic Perspectives on Women's Fear of Success." *International Forum of Psychoanalysis* 15, no. 2 (2006): 85–95. doi: 10.1080/08037060600621779.

Ryan, R. and Deci, E. L. "Intrinsic and Extrinsic Motivations: Classic Definitions and New Directions." *Contemporary Educational Psychology* 25, no. 1 (2000): 54–67. doi: 10.1006/ceps.1999.1020.

Substance Abuse and Mental Health Services Administration. "The Eight Dimensions of Wellness." U.S. Department of Health and Human Services. Updated October 24, 2017. https://www.samhsa.gov/wellness-initiative/eight-dimensions-wellness.

Salmon, T.W. "Mental Hygiene." *American Journal of Public Health* 96, no. 10 (2006): 1740–42. https://www.ncbi.nlm.nih.gov/pmc/articles/ PMC1586143.

Sanchez-Reilly, S., Morrison, L. J., Carey, E. et al. "Caring for Oneself to Care for Others: Physicians and Their Self-Care." *The Journal of Supportive Oncology* 11, no. 2 (2013): 75–81. https://www.ncbi.nlm.nih.gov/pubmed/23967495.

Schmidt, A. M. and DeShon, R. P. "What to Do? The Effects of Discrepancies, Incentives, and Time on Dynamic Goal Prioritization." *Journal of Applied Psychology* 92, no. 4 (2007): 928–41. doi: 10.1037/0021-9010.92.4.928.

Schott, R. M. *Cognition and Eros: A Critique of the Kantian Paradigm.* University Park: Pennsylvania State University Press, 1993.

Schunk, D. H. "Social Cognitive Theory and Self-Regulated Learning." In *Self-Regulated Learning and Academic Achievement: Theoretical Perspectives,* 2nd ed., edited by B. J. Zimmerman and D. H. Schunk. Mahwah, NJ: Erlbaum, 2001.

Schwinger, M., Wirthwein, L., Lemmer, G. et al. "Academic Self-Handicapping and Achievement: a Meta-Analysis." *Journal of Educational Psychology* 106, no. 3 (2014): 744–761. doi: 10.1037/a0035832

Scullin, M. K., Krueger, M. L., Ballard, H. K. et al. "The Effects of Bedtime Writing on Difficulty Falling Asleep: A Polysomnographic Study Comparing To-Do Lists and Completed Activity Lists." *Journal of Experimental Psychology: General* 147, no. 1 (2018): 139–46. doi: 10.1037/xge0000374.

Seligman, M. E. P. *Helplessness: On Depression, Development, and Death.* San Francisco: W. H. Freeman, 1975.

Sheldon, K. M. and Elliot, A. J. "Not All Personal Goals Are Personal: Comparing Autonomous and Controlled Reasons as Predictors of Effort and Attainment." *Personality and Social Psychology Bulletin* 24, no. 5 (1998): 546–57. doi: 10.1177/0146167298245010.

Singh, S. and Sharma, N. R. "Self-Regulation as a Correlate of Psychological Well-Being." *Indian Journal of Health and Wellbeing* 9, no. 3 (2018): 441–44.

Sexton, J. D., Pennebaker, J. W., Holzmueller, C. G. et al. "Care for the Caregiver: Benefits of Expressive Writing for Nurses in the United States." *Progress in Palliative Care* 17, no. 6 (2009): 307–12. doi: 10.1179/096992609X12455871937620.

Sternberg, R. J. "Self-Sabotage in the Academic Career." *Chronicle of Higher Education.* April 29, 2013. https://www.chronicle.com/article/Self-Sabotage-in-the-Academic/138875.

Strouse, S. *Artful Grief: A Diary of Healing.* Bloomington, IN: Balboa Press, 2013.

Sweeny, K. and Howell, J. L. "Bracing Later and Coping Better: Benefits of Mindfulness During a Stressful Waiting Period." *Personality and Social Psychology Bulletin* 43, no. 10 (2017): 1399–1414. doi: 10.1177/0146167217713490.

Swetz, K. M., Harrington, S. E., Matsuyama, R. K. et al. "Strategies for Avoiding Burnout in Hospice and Palliative Medicine: Peer Advice for Physicians on Achieving Longevity and Fulfillment." *Journal of Palliative Medicine* 12, no. 9 (2009): 773–77. doi: 10.1089/jpm.2009.0050.

Tapper, K. "Mindfulness and Craving: Effects and Mechanisms." *Clinical Psychology Review* 59 (2018): 10117. doi: 10.1016/j.cpr.2017.11.003.

University of London. "Self-Esteem Map in the Human Brain." October 24, 2017. https://www.sciencedaily.com/releases/2017/10/171024103319.htm.

University of Surrey. "Sharing Experiences Improves Well-Being of Healthcare Staff." October 27, 2017. www.sciencedaily.com/releases/2017/10/171027090159.htm.

Ussher, M., Spatz, A., Copland, C., Nicolaou, A. et al. "Immediate Effects of a Brief Mindfulness-Based Body Scan on Patients with Chronic Pain." *Journal of Behavioral Medicine* 37, no. 1 (2014): 127–134. doi: 10.1007/s10865-012-9466-5.

Vail, K. E., Juhl, J., Arndt, M. et al. "When Death Is Good for Life: Considering the Positive Trajectories of Terror Management." *Personality and Social Psychology Review* 16, no. 4 (2012): 303–29. doi: 10 1177/1088868312440046.

van Harmelen, A., Gibson, J. L., St Clair, M. C. et al. "Friendships and Family Support Reduce Subsequent Depressive Symptoms in At-Risk Adolescents." *PLOS ONE* 11, no. 5 (2016): e0153715. doi: 10 1371/journal.pone.0153715.

Vann, R. J., Rosa, J. A., McCrea, S. M. "When Consumers Struggle: Action Crisis and Its Effects on Problematic Goal Pursuit." *Psychology and Marketing* 35, no. 9 (2018): 696–709. doi: 10.1002/mar.21116.

Watanabe, A. "Relationship between Four Components of Assertiveness and Mental Health among High School Students." *Japanese Journal of Psychology* 80, no. 1 (2009): 48–53. doi: 10.4992/jpsy.80.48.

White, M. A., Mayer, M., Vanderlind, W. M. et al. "Evaluation of a Behavioral Self-Care Intervention for Public Health Students." *American Journal of Health Education* 49, no. 1 (2018): 40–47. doi: 10.1080/19325037.2017.1369199.

World Health Organization. "10 Facts on Mental Health." 2018. http://www.who.int/features/factfiles/mental_health/mental_health_facts/en.

Yavuzer, Y. "Investigating the Relationship between Self-Handicapping Tendencies, Self-Esteem and Cognitive Distortions." *Educational Sciences: Theory and Practice* 15, no. 4 (2015): 879–90. doi: 10.12738/estp.2015.4.2434.

ACKNOWLEDGMENTS

Throughout my life, I have been fortunate to have been surrounded by positive individuals who have encouraged me to follow my dreams. I am indebted to my husband, Evan, for his unwavering support and empowerment throughout this journey. I am grateful for my family and friends, who have been loving cheerleaders throughout this endeavor. Many thanks to the Ulysses Press team for sharing your talent with me in this project. Finally, thank you warmly to my clients, who allow me to witness their inspirational courage and dedication as they improve their self-love and overall well-being.

ABOUT THE AUTHOR

Dr. Shainna Ali is a mental health clinician, educator, and advocate who is dedicated to highlighting the important role of mental health in fostering happiness, fulfillment, and overall wellness. She is the owner of Integrated Counseling Solutions, a counseling and consulting practice in central Florida. In her practice, she uses a strengths-based approach that empowers clients on their journey of self-love. Within the field of mental health, her areas of expertise include exploring identity and culture, fostering emotional intelligence, healing from trauma, and utilizing creative counseling methods. When she isn't working, she invests in her self-love by practicing yoga, spending time with her loved ones, teaching dance, or exploring the world.

Dr. Shainna enjoys advocating for the importance of self-love and mental health at workshops and presentations, in the media, and through her *Psychology Today*–hosted blog, *A Modern Mentality*. She has been named 30 under 30 by her alma mater, The University of Central Florida, highlighted as an emerging leader by the Association of Counselor Education and Supervision, and honored with the Pete Fischer Humanitarian Award by the Florida Counseling Association.

Printed in the USA
CPSIA information can be obtained
at www.ICGtesting.com
CBHW080541210424
7177CB00007B/100